THE RESPONSIBILITY OF THE PRIESTS IN THE TABERNACLE

CASSANDRA BROADNAX

WESTBOW
PRESS®
A DIVISION OF THOMAS NELSON
& ZONDERVAN

WestBow Press books may be ordered through booksellers or by contacting:

WestBow Press
A Division of Thomas Nelson & Zondervan
1663 Liberty Drive
Bloomington, IN 47403
www.westbowpress.com
844-714-3454

All citations taken from the Hebrew-Greek Key Word Study Bible
Spiros Zodhiates, Th.D.
1984, 1991 by AMG International, Inc. Revised Edition 1991

ISBN: 979-8-3850-2785-9 (sc)
ISBN: 979-8-3850-2786-6 (hc)
ISBN: 979-8-3850-2787-3 (e)

Library of Congress Control Number: 2024912534

Print information available on the last page.

WestBow Press rev. date: 07/11/2024

CONTENTS

Foreword. vii

1   The Designation and Responsibility of the Priests 1

2   Instructions in Transporting the Tabernacle
     and Its Vessels 11

3   Three Tabernacles. 23

4   The Altar of Burnt Offering 39

5   The Brazen Laver 55

6   The Golden Candlestick 63

7   The Table of Shewbread. 69

8   The Altar of Incense. 75

9   The Ark of the Covenant and the Mercy Seat 83

10   The Ministry of Cherubim 93

11   The Garment of the Priests. 103

12   Jesus, the Fulfillment of the Tabernacle and the Law . . . 111

I began writing this book after being in ministry for almost twenty years. In 2014 I was reading the book of Romans and in the first chapter Paul says that he is a servant of Jesus Christ, called to be an apostle, separated unto the gospel of God.

What caught my attention was the words 'gospel of God.' I had been taught that it is the gospel of Jesus Christ! Again in 1 Timothy chapter one verse eleven and 1 Thessalonians chapter one verses eight and nine, Paul said, "The gospel of God". What is the gospel of God?

I had been taught in Bible School that the word gospel means good news; the gospel is the life, death, and resurrection of Jesus Christ. But a person being hung on a cross, even if for my sins, did not sound like good news to me. Although He taught the gospel Jesus never taught the people about His life, death, and resurrection. After understanding this I was determined to find out what is the gospel of God.

I prayed and asked God to reveal to me the true gospel. He said that the preaching that the church calls the gospel today is the second half of the gospel. The life, death, and resurrection of Jesus Christ are about repentance, which is required to be delivered out of oppression. He gave me this verse:

> And almost all things are by the law purged with blood: and without blood is no remission. (Hebrews 9:22).

Another way of saying it is, And almost all things are by the law cleansed with the blood of the lamb: without the blood, there is no forgiveness of sin; without the forgiveness of sin, there is no deliverance.

Then He took me to Galatians chapter three verse eighteen where it tells us that God first preached the gospel to Abraham. God made me understand from the book of Genesis that He sent Abraham into the land of Canaan to preach the gospel. He said, The words in Genesis chapter 12 verses 1—3 is not the gospel, but the blessing Abraham would receive for being obedience to go and preach the gospel in Canaan.

Was Abraham successful? Yes, he was. He trained 318 in spiritual warfare. For 318 men to be bold enough to be willing to go up against a king who possibly had at least three thousand men conveys to me that Abraham had taught them how to have a relationship with God. To understand that they didn't fight against one king, but against four kings, tells me that Abraham's men were fearless and were well acquainted with God.

"What did God preach to Abraham? I wanted to know the exact words." What was this message that would cause a person to become bold and fearless?

I searched the entire book of Genesis, even the story of Noah, but I did not find it. I went to the sermons of Jesus in the New Testament; neither did I see it there. Then I stopped searching and went back to my daily reading of the Bible. I came to the book of Exodus and read about Moses at the burning bush. After I read the first ten verses, the Lord told me to read a second time. I read it, and He said, This is the gospel message. This is the message I sent Moses to give to the children of Israel in Egypt; this is the same message I've sent to be preached from Genesis to Revelations. My word does not change.

I found out what the gospel message is, and then I asked, Why does the church today teach that Jesus Christ and Him crucified is the gospel? The Lord said to me, It is taught because my ministers do not believe that the Old Testament is relevant today. But when Jesus was on the earth there was no New Testament, He and His disciples after His ascension had only the Old Testament to study and reference from. The case today for ministers is much like that of the children of Israel as they traveled through the wilderness knowing only the acts of God and not His ways; as David said in (Psalm 103:7).

The Lord said to me, To know my ways as well as my acts you must read, study, and meditate on the Old Testament daily, just as I commanded Joshua. I commanded Moses to write several special instruction books to those I have called into ministry, the books of Leviticus and Malachi. Without the understanding of these two books those who are called will never reach the position of being 'sent.' Only those who are sent have their feet shod with the preparation of the gospel of peace. I choose them, they are not chosen by man.

The book of Leviticus explains the process of offering sacrifice and the different types of sacrifices. The book of Malachi warns of the curses they may receive for not following God's instructions properly and how to correct them.

Often when we are told that Jesus died for our sins, we only see in our minds a picture of Jesus hanging on the cross; we don't see the process of getting there. Leviticus explains the process, not just what the lamb went through, but the responsibility of the priest and the offeror. The offeror came to repent of his sins, the priest was there to instruct him and to finish the process after the offeror had cut the animal's throat. The Lamb said nothing, and did nothing; it was the priest and the offeror who went through the process. It is the same process today only in a new and living way.

You see it again in Exodus chapter twelve verses one through twenty-eight, but more so from the perspective of the offeror. The children of Israel were acting in faith; they simply obeyed God's instructions to kill the lamb, not understanding that they were offering sacrifices. They went through the process of repentance.

This is just as a person who has decided to give their life to Christ; not knowing the process he follows the instructions of the minister to repent.

God sent Moses with the gospel message of deliverance, but before they could be delivered, they had to repent of their sins and dedicate their lives to God. You ask, What were their sins? Ezekiel chapter twenty tells us while they were in Egypt they had been worshiping the idols of Egypt. They confessed their sin by removing the leaven from their homes; for leaven is what was used in the bread which was offered to the idols. They dedicated their lives to God by killing the lamb and burning the entire animal. They renounced the idols and confessed God as their Lord by placing the blood of the lamb upon the doorpost.

Jesus said, To whom much is given, much is required (Luke 12:48). One who has been called into ministry by God has been given a great responsibility. It is our responsibility to seek God's kingdom to learn what it is, what it is about, and how to operate in it. Then we are to know what His righteousness is and operate accordingly. We must allow it to work in our own lives before we can teach others, in doing so we become examples, testimonies of the truth of God's word, and His goodness.

To say that the life, death, and resurrection of Jesus Christ is the gospel is the same as Ahimaaz the son of Zadok going to David with half the message. Although Joab told Ahimaaz he didn't have a message, he wanted to go because he could run faster than Cushi. Ahimaaz could only tell David that they had won the battle, he could not inform him of any other details concerning the battle.

It is vitally important that every minister of the gospel fully understand the message of the gospel, the office of a minister, and the responsibility of the office. It does not matter whether you have been called to be an apostle, a prophet, an evangelist, a pastor, or a teacher you are a minister, an administrator, not a gift to the church; and should be grounded in the truth. It is vital that not knowing the truth of the gospel leads to the death of the church.

Not fully understanding all of our responsibilities as ministers of the gospel is the same as allowing the locust, the cankerworm, the caterpillar, and the palmerworm which slowly destroy the church; little things that slowly eat away different parts of the tree until it dies.

God is calling forth an army who will boldly stand for truth just as Elijah did in his generation, just as John the Baptist did in his generation. We have been called forth to restore 'all things' as Jesus said to His disciples (Matthew 17:10—13). It begins with understanding and knowing the responsibility of the priests.

CHAPTER ONE

THE DESIGNATION AND RESPONSIBILITY OF THE PRIESTS

Jacob, the son of Isaac, married and had twelve sons and one daughter (Genesis 29:15–35; 30:1–24 KJV).

The third son's name is Levi, which means joined. From birth the tribe of Levi was designated to be joined unto God. Levi had three sons, Gershon, Merari, and Kohath. All of them were priests, but the sons of Aaron, the son of Kohath, were high priests; Moses and Aaron were the sons of Kohath.

In Exodus 3, God chooses Moses of the tribe of Levi to deliver the children of Israel out of Egypt. In chapter 4 God chooses Aaron the brother of Moses to go with Moses.

In Exodus 20, God reveals Himself to the children of Israel and gives to them Ten Commandments. He commands them not to worship idols and to love and respect one another, but they reject God. Then Moses goes up on the mount to talk with God.

Moses returns from receiving the Ten Commandments written on two stones and finds the children of Israel worshipping a golden calf, and he destroys the calf with fire and water. After he destroys the idol, Moses says to the children of Israel, "Who is on the Lord's side? Let him come unto me" (Exod. 32:26). After all the sons of Levi gather together, Moses commands the tribe of Levi to slay those men who had worshipped the golden calf.

In Numbers 25, God is angry with the children of Israel because they have joined themselves unto the god of the Moabites, Baal-peor, by committing whoredom with the daughters of Moab during their yearly feast. God is so angry that He commands Moses to hang all the men who had joined themselves to Baal-peor. While Moses is giving instructions to the judges, one of the young men enters the camp with one of the Moabite women and takes her to his tent.

Phinehas, the son of Eleazar, the son of Aaron the priest, gets very angry, goes into the tent, and slays both the young man and the woman. For this the Lord gives not only to Phinehas but also to Phinehas's children a covenant of peace, because he has been zealous for the Lord among the children of Israel.

The book of Malachi is written to the priests, not to the people. In it, God rebukes the priests and puts a curse upon them for accepting sacrifices with blemishes, as well as for not knowing and rejecting His statutes, laws, and judgments. In chapter 2, God confirms that He has not only made a covenant with Phinehas, but also with the whole tribe of Levi.

The Old Testament points to the fact that God would send a man not of the tribe of Levi, but of Juda, who would be the one to deliver His people out of bondage, Christ Jesus. Today God chooses a man or woman not because of the tribe they are from, but because of their character and personality.

The designation to become a priest of God is given to him before he is in his mother's womb. He says to Jeremiah, "Before I formed thee in the belly I knew thee, and before thou camest forth out of the womb I sanctified thee, and I ordained thee a prophet unto the nations" (Jer. 1:5).

First God calls us to the office. It is up to each man or woman to accept or reject that appointment when we come of age. God will not force you to do His will. If we accept that appointment,

He tries us to see how studious and faithful we will be. Third, if we pass the test then He chooses you to the office. Jesus says, "For many are called, but few are chosen" (Matt. 22:14). Another word for being chosen is to be sent. "And how shall they preach, except they be sent? As it is written, How beautiful are the feet of them that preach the gospel of peace, and bring glad tidings of good things!" (Rom. 10:15).

Whenever a product is created, the manufacturer will test the product before putting it on the market to sell. Likewise, God tests each of us to see whether we will work properly according to His will. Simply being called into ministry does not mean that God has chosen someone to shepherd His people. God will not send you forward until you are properly prepared; this ordination comes with great responsibility because there are lives at stake. Jesus says, "For unto whomsoever much is given, of him shall be much required: and to whom men have committed much, of him they will ask the more" (Luke 12:48).

Jesus is called by God into ministry, baptized by John the Baptist, filled with the Holy Spirit, and led by the Spirit into the wilderness to be tested. It is after He passes the test that He is sent to fulfill His ministry. If Jesus is subject to the test of God, every minister who accepts God's call will be as well.

The first part of the test is to know the voice of God. How do you know that God called you into ministry? If another person told you that you have been called, then you are not ready. It is only when you know that God Himself called you that you are ready to begin. God called Abraham. God called Moses. God called Jeremiah and each of the prophets; they all knew His voice. God speaks to us by His Spirit, His still small voice. It was the Spirit of God who led Jesus into the wilderness.

The second part of the test is to know God's word. After you have accepted God's call, you will become responsible for reading and studying God's written word. God said to Joshua, "This book of the law shall not depart out of thy mouth; but thou shalt meditate therein day and night, that thou mayest observe to do according to all that is written therein: for then thou shalt make thy way prosperous, and then thou shalt have good success" (Josh. 1:8).

When Jesus is twelve years old, the Bible says, He increases in wisdom and stature, as well as in favor with God and man. Also, when He is in the wilderness being tempted by the devil, His only weapon is the word of God, and according to Ephesians 6, God's word in you becomes the sword of the Spirit.

It is the responsibility of the priests to know the tabernacle: what it means, how to operate in it, how to minister to God and to the people. The people enter into the gate of the tabernacle and are permitted to go no further than before the burnt altar. But the priests are permitted to enter into the Holy Place and into the Holy of Holies, into the very presence of God.

The responsibility of the priests is seen in the way the vessels of the tabernacle and the tabernacle itself are transported. The burnt altar, table of showbread, altar of incense, and the ark are equipped with staves (poles), which are carried upon the shoulders of the priests. To carry something on your shoulders means to take responsibility for it and its purpose.

When Jesus begins His ministry, He calls disciples to walk with Him, to become students. It is after they had been with Him for some time, as He ministers unto the people, that He chooses them, gives them authority, and calls them apostles—even those He knows will become afraid and be sifted by Satan and betray Him. He knows who will stand with great boldness to do the will of God.

In the Old Testament, not only are the priests, the Levites, responsible for knowing and understanding the tabernacle, but the prophets called by God who were not of the tribe of Levi know and understand the tabernacle and how to operate in it. They know the physical building as well as the spiritual function of it.

You cannot understand the ministry of Jesus until you understand the tabernacle and the ministry of the priests in the tabernacle. You see, there was no New Testament when Jesus began His ministry; He preached, taught, and ministered just as the priests in the Old Testament. It was the new and living way in which He ministered that was written after He had ascended to heaven that became the New Testament.

Many want to say that the Old Testament is done away with, but that is not what Jesus says:

> *Think not that I am come to destroy the law, or the prophets: I am not come to destroy, but to fulfill.*
>
> *For verily I say unto you, Till heaven and earth pass, one jot or one tittle shall in no wise pass from the law, till all be fulfilled.*
>
> *Whosoever therefore shall break one of these least commandments, and shall teach men so, he shall be called the least in the kingdom of heaven: but whosoever shall do and teach them, the same shall be called great in the kingdom of heaven.*
>
> *For I say unto you, That except your righteousness shall exceed the righteousness of the scribes and Pharisees, ye shall in no case enter into the kingdom of heaven.* (Matt. 5:17–20)

> *And He said unto them, These are the words which I spake unto you, while I was with you, that all thing must be fulfilled, which were written in the law of Moses, and in the prophets, and in the Psalms, concerning me.* (Luke 24:44)

> *Then said He unto them, Therefore every scribe which is instructed unto the kingdom of heaven is like unto a man that is a householder, which bringeth forth out of his treasure things new and old.* (Matt. 13:52)

You cannot continually read one book of the Bible or only certain verses of the Bible and war against the enemy. You study to show yourself approved, knowing the whole word of God. You cannot simply take the face value of what you read; you must find the meaning and relevance of what you read. You must understand why God said what He said.

Some people say that because the old covenant was completely done away with, we don't have to obey it, not understanding that it was not done away with but was amended by God improving it. Much wisdom is found when we learn why God amended it.

> *Behold, the days come, saith the Lord, that I will make a new covenant with the house of Israel and with the house of Judah:*
>
> *Not according to the covenant that I made with their fathers in the day I took them by the hand to bring them out of the land of Egypt; which my covenant they broke, although I was a husband unto them, saith the Lord:*
>
> *But this shall be the covenant that I will make with the house of Israel; After those days, saith the Lord, I will put my law in their inward parts, and write it in their hearts; and will be their God, and they shall be my people.*
>
> *And they shall teach no more every man his neighbor, and every man his brother, saying, Know the Lord: for they shall all know me, from the least of them unto the greatest of them, saith the Lord: for I will forgive their iniquity, and I will remember their sin no more.* (Jer. 31:31–34)

> *For if that first covenant had been faultless, then should no place have been sought for the second.*

For finding fault with them, He saith, Behold, the days come, saith the Lord, when I will make a new covenant with the house of Israel and with the house of Judah:

Not according to the covenant that I made with their fathers in the day when I took them by the hand to lead them out of the land of Egypt; because they continued not in my covenant, and I regarded them not, saith the Lord.

For this is the covenant that I will make with the house of Israel after those days, saith the Lord; I will put my laws into their mind, and write them in their hearts: and I will be to them a God, and they shall be to me a people:

And they shall not teach every man his neighbor, and every man his brother, saying, Know the Lord: for all shall know me, from the least to the greatest.

For I will be merciful to their unrighteousness, and their sins and their iniquities will I remember no more.

In that He saith, A new covenant, He hath made the first old. Now that which is decayed and waxed old is ready to vanish away. (Heb. 8:7–13)

Then verily the first covenant had also ordinances of divine service, and a worldly sanctuary.

For there was a tabernacle made; the first, whereon was the candlestick, and the table, and the showbread; which is called the sanctuary. (Heb. 9:1–2)

The first covenant was physical, written on stone, and kept in a tabernacle; its ministry could be seen with the eye. The second is in the mind of man, written in his heart, and spiritual. Hebrews 9 tells us that the first was a figure for the time then present. The word *figure* means symbolic: it was symbolic of what was to come.

If the first was worldly, the second in the body of man, then the third is spiritual. The third tabernacle Moses saw in heaven, in the spirit: And thou shalt rear up the tabernacle according to the fashion thereof which was showed thee in the mount (Exod. 26:30).

Yet even within the tabernacle God made changes in the ministry of the priests at different times. Let us look at the changes He made. Note that it was God who wrote the covenant, and only God can change them according to His will.

In the book of Exodus, God gives to Moses specific instructions for the priests, who alone are responsible for transporting the tabernacle and its vessels. Once David becomes king over Israel and has taken possession of all the land given to Israel by God, He tries to bring the ark of God into Jerusalem. But in the process, one of the young men transporting the ark is killed.

For three months David searches the scriptures to find out why God has killed Uzza. He finds the answer: only the high priests were to carry the ark, the priests had to be sanctified, and they had to carry the ark in the specific manner instructed by God. As David studies the word of God, he is also given a revelation of the ministry of the tabernacle, a change in the will of God. He understands that the priests no longer have to transport the vessels of the tabernacle, because the children of Israel had arrived in the Promised Land; therefore, there was no reason to transport the tabernacle leaving some priests without a ministry—or so it seemed.

In 1 Chronicles, God reveals to David by the Spirit that he should assign these priests to be musicians, singers, door keepers, porters, secretaries, record keepers, and members of a finance department in the tabernacle. God reveals to him that this is the same as carrying the tabernacle and its vessels.

Once John the Baptist's and Jesus's ministry begin, another change happens. The temple is no longer stationary, but mobile again. For man's body becomes the temple of God: "What? Know ye not that your body is the temple of the Holy Ghost which is in you, which ye have of God, and ye are not your own?" (1 Cor. 6:19). From this we understand that we are looking at three tabernacles: the tabernacle of God in heaven, the tabernacle of Moses in the physical, and the tabernacle in man. God gives to Moses a physical tabernacle for man to see that he might understand what he cannot see. They all operate in the same manner.

Therefore, it is extremely important that every minister of the gospel of Jesus Christ know and understand the three forms of the tabernacle and its ministry.

CHAPTER TWO

INSTRUCTIONS IN TRANSPORTING THE TABERNACLE AND ITS VESSELS

And they shall make an ark of shittim wood: two cubits and a half shall be the length thereof, and a cubit and a half the breadth thereof, and a cubit and a half the height thereof.

And thou shalt overlay it with pure gold, within and without shalt thou overlay it, and shalt make upon it a crown of gold round about.

And thou shalt cast four rings of gold for it, and put them in the four corners thereof; and two rings shall be in the one side of it, and two rings in the other side of it.

And thou shalt make staves of shittim wood, and overlay them with gold.

And thou shalt put the staves into the rings by the sides of the ark, that the ark may be borne with them [carried on the shoulders].

The staves shall be in the rings of the ark: they shall not be taken from it. (Exod. 25:10–15)

To be carried on the shoulders means responsibility; the priests are responsible for carrying the presence of God.

God allowed the tabernacle and its vessels to be transported in carts, except for the ark.

> *And it came to pass on the day that Moses had fully set up the tabernacle, and had anointed it, and sanctified it, and all the instruments thereof, both the altar and all the vessels thereof, and had anointed them, and sanctified them;*
>
> *That the princes of Israel, heads of the house of their fathers, who were the princes of the tribes, and were over them that were numbered, offered:*
>
> *And they brought their offering before the Lord, six covered wagons, and twelve oxen; a wagon for two of the princes, and for each one an ox: and they brought them before the tabernacle.*
>
> *And the Lord spake unto Moses, saying,*
>
> *Take it of them, that they may be to do the service of the tabernacle of the congregation; and thou shalt give them unto the Levites, to every man according to his service.*
>
> *And Moses took the wagons and the oxen, and gave them unto the Levites.*
>
> *Two wagons and four oxen he gave unto the sons of Gershon, according unto their service:*
>
> *And four wagons and eight oxen he gave unto the sons of Merari, according unto their service, under the hand of Ithamar the son of Aaron the priest.*
>
> *But unto the sons of Kohath he gave none: because the service of the sanctuary belonging unto them was that they should bear upon their shoulders.* (Num. 7:1–9)

God commanded that the ark be carried in a particular manner: only by the high priest and his sons. At the same time, the priests carrying the ark had to be sanctified and had to understand the purpose of the ark. If not, they would die.

Death resulted when the priests carrying the ark were unclean.

And the word of Samuel came to all Israel. Now Israel went out against the Philistines to battle, and pitched beside Eben-ezer: and the Philistines pitched in Aphek.

And the Philistines put themselves in array against Israel: and when they joined battle, Israel was smitten before the Philistines: and they slew of the army in the field about four thousand men.

And when the people were come into the camp, the elders of Israel said, Wherefore hath the Lord smitten us to day before the Philistines? Let us fetch the ark of the covenant of the Lord out of Shiloh unto us, that, when it cometh among us, it may save us out of the hand of our enemies.

So the people sent to Shiloh, that they might bring from thence the ark of the covenant of the Lord of hosts, which dwelleth between the cherubims: and the two son of Eli, Hophni and Phinehas, were there with the ark of the covenant of God.

And when the ark of the covenant of the Lord came into the camp, all Israel shouted with a great shout, so that the earth rang again. (1 Sam. 4:1–5)

In 1 Samuel, it says, "And the ark of God was taken; and the two sons of Eli, Hophni and Phinehas, were slain." Later chapters speak of other sons of high priests who carried the ark but carried it in the proper manner: "Zadok therefore and Abiathar carried the ark of God again to Jerusalem: and they tarried there." (2 Sam. 15:29).

Death resulted when the high priests carried the ark without wisdom.

> *So David gathered all Israel together, from Shihor of Egypt even unto the entering of Hemath, to bring the ark of God from Kirjath-jearim.*
>
> *And David went up, and all Israel, to Baalah, that is, to Judah, to bring up thence the ark of God the Lord, that dwelleth between the cherubims, whose name is called on it.*
>
> *And they carried the ark of God in a new cart out of the house of Abinadab: and Uzza and Ahio drove the cart.*
>
> *And David and all Israel played before God with all their might, and with singing, and with harps, and with psalteries, and with timbrels, and with cymbals, and with trumpets.*
>
> *And when they came unto the threshing floor of Chidon, Uzza put forth his hand to hold the ark; for the oxen stumbled.*
>
> *And the anger of the Lord was kindled against Uzza, and He smote him, because he put his hand to the ark: and there he died before God.* (1 Chron. 13:5–10)

David goes to God to find out why He has killed Uzza. In 1 Chronicles 15, after he finds the answer, David rebukes the priests for not knowing due order and commands them to sanctify themselves before bringing the ark into the city of David the second time.

> *Then David said, None ought to carry the ark of God but the Levites: for them hath the Lord chosen to carry the ark of God, and to minister unto Him forever.*

> And David gathered all Israel together to Jerusalem, to bring up the ark of the Lord unto His place, which he had prepared for it.
> And David assembled the children of Aaron, and the Levites. (1 Chron. 15:2–4)

> And David called for Zadok and Abiathar the priests, and for the Levites, for Uriel, Asaiah, and Joel, Shemaiah, and Eliel, and Amminadab,
> And said unto them, Ye are the chief of the fathers of the Levites: sanctify yourselves, both ye and your brethren, that ye may bring up the ark of the Lord God of Israel unto the place I have prepared for it.
> For because ye did it not at the first, the Lord our God made a breach upon us, for that we sought Him not after the due order.
> So the priests and the Levites sanctified themselves to bring up the ark of the Lord God of Israel.
> And the children of the Levites bare the ark upon their shoulders with the staves thereon, as Moses commanded according to the word of the Lord. (1 Chron. 15:11–15)

Today it still remains the responsibility of the high priest to carry the ark of God upon his or her shoulders. The pastor and co-pastor of a church are considered the high priests of the congregation and are responsible for bringing the presence of God into the sanctuary each Sunday (or any other day) for service. God did not give that responsibility to the praise team, nor the choir, nor the deacons, nor the mothers of the church, though even all of these should be sanctified because all of them would be considered priests or ministers.

Sanctification is to be done before the pastor begins to intercede for the service and for the congregation before they arrive. The pastor of a church should not be in his study, at home, or on the way to church during praise and worship, the opening of the service, or testimony service, but already in the sanctuary in prayer and worship.

When Jesus had to minister to a congregation, He always rose up early and went to God in prayer.

> *And in the morning, rising up a great while before day, He went out, and departed into a solitary place, and there prayed.*
>
> *And Simon and they that were with him followed after him.*
>
> *And when they had found Him, they said unto Him, All men seek for thee.*
>
> *And He said unto them, Let us go into the next towns, that I may preach there also: for therefore came I forth.*
>
> *And He preached in their synagogues throughout all Galilee, and cast out devils.* (Mark 1:35–39)

The priests were responsible for sacrifices placed on the altar. They had to know whether the offeror was coming of his own voluntary will, whether the sacrifices were offered from the heart of the offeror, and whether the sacrifice had blemishes.

The sacrifice had to be from their hearts.

> *Speak ye unto all the congregation of Israel, saying, In the tenth day of this month they shall take to them every man a lamb, according to the house of their fathers, a lamb for a house:*

And if the household be too little for the lamb, let him and his neighbor next unto his house take it according to the number of the souls; every man according to his eating shall make your count for the lamb.

Your lamb shall be without blemish, a male of the first year: ye shall take it out from the sheep, or from the goats:

And ye shall keep it up until the fourteenth day of the same month: and the whole assembly of the congregation of Israel shall kill it in the evening. (Exod. 12:3–6)

If his offering be a burnt sacrifice of the herd, let him offer a male without blemish: he shall offer it of his own voluntary will at the door of the tabernacle of the congregation before the Lord.

And he shall put his hand upon the head of the offering; and it shall be accepted for him to make atonement for him.

And he shall kill the bullock before the Lord: and the priests, Aaron's sons, shall bring the blood, and sprinkle the blood round about upon the altar that is by the door of the tabernacle of the congregation. (Lev. 1:3–5)

The priests were cursed for accepting sacrifices that were blemished.

A son honoreth his father, and a servant his master: if then I be a father, where is mine honor? And if I be a master, where is my fear? Saith the Lord of hosts unto you, O priests, that despise my name. And ye say, Wherein have we despised thy name?

Ye offer polluted bread upon mine altar; and ye say, Wherein have we polluted thee? In that ye say, The table of the Lord is contemptible.

And if ye offer the blind for sacrifice, is it not evil? And if ye offer the lame and the sick, is it not evil? Offer it now unto thy governor; will he be pleased with thee, or accept thy person? Saith the Lord of hosts.

And now, I pray you, beseech God that He will be gracious unto us: this hath been by your means: will He regard your persons? Saith the Lord of hosts.

Who is there even among you that would shut the doors for naught? Neither do ye kindle fire on mine altar for naught. I have no pleasure in you, saith the Lord of hosts, neither will I accept an offering at thy hand.

For from the rising of the sun even unto the going down of the same my name shall be great among the Gentiles; and in every place incense shall be offered unto my name, and a pure offering: for my name shall be among the heathen, saith the Lord of hosts.

But ye have profaned it, in that ye say, The table of the Lord is polluted; and the fruit thereof, even his meat, is contemptible.

Ye saith also, Behold, what a weariness it is! And ye have snuffed at it, saith the Lord of hosts; and ye brought that which was torn, and the lame, and the sick; thus ye brought an offering: should I accept this of your hand? Saith the Lord.

But cursed be the deceiver, which hath in his flock a male, and voweth, and sacrificeth unto the Lord a corrupt thing: for I am a great King, saith the Lord of hosts, and my name is dreadful among the heathen. (Mal. 1:6–14)

And now, O ye priests, this commandment is for you.

If ye will not hear, and if ye will not lay it to heart, to give glory unto my name, saith the Lord of hosts, I will even send a curse upon you, and I will curse your blessings: yea, I have cursed them already, because ye do not lay it to heart.

Behold, I will corrupt your seed, and spread dung upon your faces, even the dung of your solemn feasts; and one shall take you away with it.

And ye shall know that I have sent this commandment unto you, that my covenant might be with Levi, saith the Lord of hosts.

My covenant was with him of life and peace; and I gave them to him for the fear wherewith he feared me, and as afraid before my name.

The law of truth was in his mouth, and iniquity was not found in his lips: he walked with me in peace and equity, and did turn many away from iniquity.

For the priest's lips should keep knowledge, and they should seek the law at his mouth: for he is the messenger of the Lord of hosts.

But ye are departed out of the way; ye have caused many to stumble at the law; ye have corrupted thee covenant of Levi, saith the Lord of hosts.

Therefore have I also made you contemptible and base before all the people, according as ye have not kept my ways, but have been partial in the law.

Have we not all one father? Hath not one God created us? Why do we deal treacherously every man against his brother, by profaning the covenant of our fathers?

> *Judah hath dealt treacherously, and an abomination is committed in Israel and in Jerusalem; for Judah hath profaned the holiness of the Lord which He loved, and hath married the daughter of a strange god.*
>
> *The Lord will cut off the man that doeth this, the master and the scholar, out of the tabernacle of Jacob, and him that offereth an offering unto the Lord of hosts.* (Mal. 2:1–12)

Note too that the priests were responsible for teaching the people the statutes of God.

> *And the Lord spake unto Aaron, saying,*
>
> *Do not drink wine nor strong drink, thou, nor thy sons with thee, when ye go into the tabernacle of the congregation, lest ye die: it shall be a statute forever throughout your generations;*
>
> *And that ye may put difference between holy and unholy, and between unclean and clean;*
>
> *And that ye may teach the children of Israel all the statutes which the Lord hath spoken unto them by the hand of Moses.* (Lev. 10:8–11)

In Nehemiah 8, during the Feast of Trumpets, Ezra the scribe reads the law, but the Levites give the understanding of what he reads to the people. The Levites teach the people, and when they hear and understand, the people weep, because they realize their sin.

> *And ye shall know that I have sent this commandment unto you, that my covenant might be with Levi, saith the Lord of hosts.*

> *My covenant was with him of life and peace;*
> *and I gave them to him for the fear wherewith he*
> *feared me, and was afraid before my name.*
> *The law of truth was in his mouth, and iniquity*
> *was not found in his lips: he walked with me in*
> *peace and equity, and did turn many away from*
> *iniquity.*
> *For the priest's lips should keep knowledge, and*
> *they should seek the law at his mouth: for he is the*
> *messenger of the Lord of hosts.* (Mal. 2:4–7)

If you pay close attention in the four Gospels, Jesus indeed preaches the gospel, but He teaches every time He preaches. (See Matt. 4:23; 5–7; 13:54; 23:1–39; Mark 1:21; 1:39; 6:2; Luke 13:10; 24:44–49; John 18:19–21.)

What is He teaching? He teaches what sin is, how to avoid sin, and how to repent from sin. You see this in His first Sermon on the Mount (Matt. 5–7). He teaches His disciples to preach the same subjects. We see this in the messages of Peter (Acts 2:37–39; 3:19; 5:1–11; 1 Peter 1:13–25; 2:11–21; 4:1–11) and Paul (Romans 3:9–31; 6:1–23; 7; 10; 13:8–14; 1 Cor. 5; 6; 8; 2 Cor. 2; 12:19–21; Eph. 2:1–10; 5:21-33; 6:1-9)

Note that in Romans 13, Paul is teaching the Ten Commandments, which some today say we no longer live under because they are from the Old Testament. In Matthew 5–7, Jesus is teaching the Ten Commandments, but in more detail.

If the priests (ministers of the gospel) don't understand God's due order, the tabernacle, and ministry in the tabernacle, then their congregations will not receive salvation, healing, or deliverance.

Yet God stands all day long with His arms outstretched waiting for those whom He has called to turn back to Him in repentance and who are ready to spend quality time in God's word to learn what we don't know.

Say, "Father God, forgive me for not following Your instructions and directions. I rededicate my life to You and give You my whole heart. Show me Your righteousness and Your ways. Fill me with Your love and compassion for my brethren. I ask You to give me a hunger and thirst to know Your word, wisdom and understanding of the tabernacle, and reveal to me my responsibility as a minister in tabernacle. In Jesus name I pray, and I thank You. Amen."

What does it mean to accept blind and lame sacrifices?

The instructions God gave to the priests in the Old Testament still apply to ministers today. Every priest is responsible for knowing whether or not the sacrifice offered is without blemish. If it has blemishes, as we read in Malachi 1, God will not accept it.

God gave the priests certain prayers to have the offeror to repeat, and there were certain things the priests were to have the offeror say. When the offeror refuses to say any part of the prayer, then we know that this is a blind sacrifice. For instance, the offeror refuses to say the words, "I forgive," or they refuse to call the person or persons by name they are to forgive.

Or if the minister tells the offeror to forgive, and he responds with "But I live a prayerful life," that is what you would call a lame sacrifice. We use a similar term today: a lame excuse.

Or if the minister tells the person to forgive, and instead, they say, "I have already forgiven them," this is a blind sacrifice. The offeror believes that it is the priest who is requiring them to say the words when in fact it is God who requires it—and God whom they are talking to.

CHAPTER THREE

THREE TABERNACLES

I want to talk now about the three tabernacles mentioned in chapter 1: the heavenly tabernacle, the earthly tabernacle (Moses's tabernacle), and the tabernacle of your body.

The three tabernacles differ in their locations, but all three represent the same building. Every priest must understand how to minister in the tabernacle on earth so that what they do affects the heavenly tabernacle.

Jesus said to His disciples, "And I give unto thee the keys of the kingdom of heaven: and whatsoever thou shalt bind on earth shall be bound in heaven: and whatsoever thou shalt loose on earth shall be loosed in heaven" (Matt. 16:19). He also said in the Lord's Prayer: "Thy kingdom come, Thy will be done in earth as it is in heaven" (Matt. 6:10). What we say and do on earth will affect what happens in heaven, and what we hear from heaven and speak will affect what happens on earth.

"In heaven" here means in the spirit. Note that when the prophets in the Old Testament would say, "The hand of the Lord was upon me" or "I lifted up my eyes" or "He carried me out in the spirit"—or, for instance, when Moses and Jesus went up on the mount or a high place—it refers to them being "in the spirit."

What they saw in the spirit was the heavenly tabernacle and what was going in and around it. While in the spirit, Moses saw the heavenly tabernacle and was commanded to build an earthly tabernacle for the people to get the understanding, for they could not see in the spirit.

When John the Baptist began his ministry, he traveled; he became a portable tabernacle of God, and so did Jesus and His disciples.

THE HEAVENLY TABERNACLE

God commanded Moses to build a tabernacle according to the pattern he saw in the mount, for Moses had seen the heavenly tabernacle. The pattern had to be exactly the same.

> *And let them make me a sanctuary; that I may dwell among them.*
> *According to all that I show thee, after the pattern of the tabernacle, and the pattern of all the instruments thereof, even so shall ye make it.* (Exod. 25:8–9)

Jesus teaches that when we pray, what we hear and see in heaven should be done in earth. For the house (temple) of God is a house of prayer: "And said unto them, It is written, My house shall be called the house of prayer; but ye have made it a den of thieves" (Matt. 21:13).

In 2 Chronicles 6, King Solomon prays and makes reference to the fact that those who pray for forgiveness have either to come to the temple (same as the tabernacle) or turn in its direction.

Even though the books of the Bible do not state it, it is fact that every one of the prophets knew, understood, and operated as a minister in the tabernacle, whether there was a physical building in their location or not. Let us look at a few of them.

John the Revelator, while on the isle of Patmos, sees the throne in heaven; he sees the spiritual tabernacle and God sitting on His throne:

> *After this I looked, and, behold, a door was opened in heaven: and the first voice which I heard was as it were of a trumpet talking with me; which said, Come up hither, and I will show thee things which must be hereafter.*
>
> *And immediately I was in the spirit: and, behold, a throne was set in heaven, and one sat on the throne.*
>
> *And He that sat was to look upon like a jasper and a sardine stone: and there was a rainbow round about the throne, in sight like unto an emerald.* (Rev. 4:1–3)

Isaiah too sees the heavenly tabernacle and the Lord sitting on His throne. He sees the seraphim and the burnt altar. He sees his heart and mind being cleansed of sin after he repents:

> *In the year that king Uzziah died I saw the Lord sitting upon a throne, high and lifted up, and His train filled the temple.*
>
> *Above it stood the seraphims: each one had six wings; with twain he covered his face, and with twain he covered his feet, and with twain he did fly.*
>
> *And one cried unto another, and said, Holy, holy, holy, is the Lord of hosts: the whole earth is full of His glory.*
>
> *And the posts of the door moved at the voice of him that cried, and the house was filled with smoke.*

> *Then said I, Woe is me! For I am undone;*
> *because I am a man of unclean lips, and I dwell in*
> *the midst of a people of unclean lips: for mine eyes*
> *have seen the King, the Lord of hosts.*
>
> *Then flew one of the seraphims unto me,*
> *having a live coal in his hand, which he had taken*
> *with the tongs from off the altar:*
>
> *And he laid it upon my mouth, and said, Lo,*
> *this hath touched thy lips; and thine iniquity is*
> *taken away, and thy sin purged.* (Isa. 6:1–7)

Ezekiel sees the heavenly tabernacle and the Lord sitting upon His throne:

> *And above the firmament that was over their heads*
> *was the likeness of a throne, as the appearance of a*
> *sapphire stone: and upon the likeness of the throne*
> *was the likeness as the appearance of a man above*
> *upon it.*
>
> *And I saw as the color of amber, as the*
> *appearance of fire round about within it, from the*
> *appearance of his loins even upward, and from the*
> *appearance of His loins even downward, I saw as it*
> *were the appearance of fire, and it had brightness*
> *round about.*
>
> *As the appearance of the bow that is in the cloud*
> *in the day of rain, so was the appearance of the*
> *brightness round about. This was the appearance*
> *of the likeness of the glory of the Lord. And when*
> *I saw it, I fell upon my face, and I heard a voice of*
> *one that spake.* (Ezek. 1:26-28)

The command to build the tabernacle according to the pattern given to Moses never changes from Genesis to Revelation; from generation to generation, whether making a tent, constructing a physical building of stone, or building the temple in the heart of man, the pattern is always the same.

In 1 Chronicles 28, David gives the pattern of the temple to his son Solomon to build. In verse 19, David tells Solomon that God revealed the pattern to him while he was in the spirit, reading the word of God. He received this revelation during the three months he searched the scriptures to understand why God killed Uzza. Daniel was in Babylon, nowhere near the temple, but he prayed three times every day as if he were in the physical temple. Even Jeremiah, who is placed in a pit, prays every day as if he were in the temple.

The tabernacle or temple is not about a building, but about relationship between God and man. In the revelation of the tabernacle, man learns how to become holy so that he can come before the throne of God.

JUDGING THE TEMPLE

God also gives instructions to the prophets to judge the temple, both the building and the ministry within it. In fact, his emphasis is not so much on the building as those responsible for what happens in the temple, the priests. Where we see the Lord command a prophet to measure the temple, He is instructing the prophet to judge not the building but the leaders in the temple.

> *In the visions of God brought me into the land of Israel, and set me upon a very high mountain, by which was as the frame of a city on the south.*
>
> *And He brought me thither, and, behold, there was a man, whose appearance was like the appearance of brass, with a line of flax in his hand, and a measuring reed; and he stood in the gate.*

And the man said unto me, Son of man, behold with thine eyes, and hear with thine ears, and set thine heart upon all that I shall show thee; for to the intent that I might shew them unto thee art thou brought hither: declare all that thou seest to the house of Israel. (Ezek. 40:2–4)

I lifted up mine eyes again, and looked, and behold, a man with a measuring line in his hand.

Then said I, Whither goest thou? And he said unto me, To measure Jerusalem, to see what is the breadth thereof, and what is the length thereof.

And, behold, the angel that talked with me went forth, and another angel went out to meet him,

And said unto him, Run, speak to this young man, saying, Jerusalem shall be inhabited as towns without walls for the multitude of men and cattle therein:

For I, saith the Lord, will be unto her a wall of fire round about, and will be the glory in the midst of her. (Zech. 2:1–5)

And there was given me a reed like unto a rod: and the angel stood, saying, Rise, and measure the temple of God, and the altar, and them that worship therein.

But the court which is without the temple leave out, and measure it not; for it is given unto the Gentiles: and the holy city shall they tread under foot forty and two months. (Rev. 11:1–2)

Paul reveals to us what it means to measure:

It is reported commonly that there is fornication among you, and such fornication as is not so much as named among the Gentiles, that one should have his father's wife.

And ye are puffed up, and have not rather mourned, that he that hath done this deed might be taken away from among you.

For I verily, as absent in body, but present in spirit, have judged already, as though I were present, concerning him that hath so done this deed.

In the name of our Lord Jesus Christ, when ye are gathered together, and my spirit, with the power of our Lord Jesus Christ,

To deliver such a one unto Satan for the destruction of the flesh, that the spirit may be saved in the day of the Lord Jesus.

Your glorying is not good. Know ye not that a little leaven leaveneth the whole lump?

Purge out therefore the old leaven, that ye may be a new lump, as ye are unleavened. For even Christ our Passover is sacrificed for us:

Therefore let us keep the feast, not with old leaven, neither with the leaven of malice and wickedness; but with the unleavened bread of sincerity and truth.

I wrote unto you in an epistle not to company with fornicators:

Yet not altogether with the fornicators of this world, or with the covetous, or extortioners, or with idolaters; for then must ye needs go out of the world.

But now I have written unto you not to keep company, if any man that is called a brother be a fornicator, or covetous, or an idolator, or a railer, or a drunkard, or an extortioner; with such a one no not to eat.

> *For what have I to do to judge them also that*
> *are without? Do not ye judge them that are within?*
> *But them that are without God judgeth.*
> *Therefore put away from among yourselves that*
> *wicked person.* (1 Cor. 5:1–13)

THE EARTHLY TABERNACLE

The vision of the earthly tabernacle is seen in the tabernacle God commands Moses to build:

> *And let them make me a sanctuary; that I may*
> *dwell among them.*
> *According to all that I show thee, after the*
> *pattern of the tabernacle, and the pattern of all*
> *the instruments thereof, even so shall ye make it.*
> (Exod. 25:8–9)

The earthly tabernacle is a figure for the time then present of the heavenly tabernacle.

> *Then verily the first covenant had also ordinances*
> *of divine service, and a worldly sanctuary.*
> *For there was a tabernacle made: the first,*
> *wherein was the candlestick, and the table, and the*
> *shewbread which is called the sanctuary.* (Heb. 9:1–2)

> *Which was a figure for the time then present, in*
> *which were offered both gifts and sacrifices, that*
> *could not make him that did the service perfect, as*
> *pertaining to the conscience.*
> *Which stood only in meats and drinks, and*
> *divers washings, and carnal ordinances, imposed*
> *on them until the time of reformation.* (Heb. 9:9–10)

THE TABERNACLE OF YOUR BODY

Once Jesus Christ ascends to heaven, He sends God's Holy Spirit to dwell in our hearts. Because the Spirit of God dwells in us, sitting upon the throne of our heart, we become the temple of God.

> *Jesus answered and said unto him, If a man love me, he will keep my words: and my Father will love him, and we will come unto him, and make our abode with him.* (John 14:23)

> *Know ye not that ye are the temple of God, and that the Spirit of God dwelleth in you?*
> *If any man defile the temple of God, him shall God destroy; for the temple of God is holy, which temple ye are.* (1 Cor. 3:16–17)

> *But the anointing which ye have received of Him abideth in you, and ye need not that any man teach you: but as the same anointing teacheth you of all things, and is truth, and is no lie, even as it hath taught you, ye shall abide in Him.*
> *And now, little children, abide in Him; that when He shall appear, we may have confidence, and not be ashamed before Him at His coming.* (1 John 2:27–28)

The tabernacle holds the keys to ministry: in worship and service to God, as well as in ministry to God's people.

How can one say that there is no need to study the tabernacle? Not studying the tabernacle and its ministry is like saying that there is no need to find out who Jesus is. For Jesus is the tabernacle. He is the tent, He is the covering, He is the door, He is every vessel of the tabernacle, He is the high priest, He is the sacrifice, the Lamb of God, He is the King of Kings!

To understand the tabernacle, you must be filled with the Spirit of God and change the way you think by the renewing of your mind. Through the study of the tabernacle you will be transformed and begin to understand what is going on in the spirit even though you cannot see it.

It is similar to a pregnant woman who has to change the way she eats, sleeps, and cares for herself. Although neither she nor anyone else can see the baby inside of her, she knows the child is there and is alive because she can feel the child. Although not many can see in the spirit, all Christians can hear and feel what is going on.

Next we will study the different parts of the tabernacle, beginning with the gate and the foundation of the wall. Although the tabernacle of Moses has only one entrance, the pattern David gives to Solomon has four walls with twelve gates. Yet the order in which God tells Moses to command the children of Israel to camp about the tabernacle has indeed walls with twelve gates.

> *Moreover thou shalt make the tabernacle with ten curtains of fine twined linen, and blue, and purple, and scarlet: with cherubims of cunning work shalt thou make them.*
>
> *The length of one curtain shall be eight and twenty cubits, and the breadth of one curtain four cubits: and every one of the curtains shall have one measure.* (Exod. 26:1–2)

> *And thou shalt make a hanging for the door of the tent, of blue, and purple, and scarlet, and fine twined linen, wrought with needlework.*

> *And thou shalt make for the hanging five pillars*
> *of shittim wood, and overlay them with gold, and*
> *their hooks shall be of gold: and thou shalt cast five*
> *sockets of brass for them.* (Exod. 26:36–37)

> *And the children of Israel shall pitch their tents,*
> *every man by his own camp, and every man by his*
> *own standard, throughout their hosts.*
> *But the Levites shall pitch round about the*
> *tabernacle of testimony, that there be no wrath*
> *upon the congregation of the children of Israel: and*
> *the Levites shall keep the charge of the tabernacle*
> *of testimony.* (Num. 1:52–53)

> *And the Lord spake unto Moses and unto Aaron,*
> *saying,*
> *Every man of the children of Israel shall pitch*
> *by his own standard, with the ensign of their*
> *father's house: far off about the tabernacle of the*
> *congregation shall they pitch.* (Num. 2:1–2)

The rest of Numbers 2 tells us that the tribes of Judah, Issachar, and Zebulun pitch on the east; Reuben, Simeon, and Gad pitch on the south; Ephraim, Manasseh, and Benjamin pitch on the west; and Asher, Dan, and Naphtali pitch on the north. The Levites encamp around about the tabernacle tent with the high priests Aaron and his sons, as well as Moses, who pitches directly in front of the gate of the tent.

John tells us that the camp was a city in the shape of a cross, with the temple at its center, called the holy Jerusalem.

> *And there came unto me one of the seven angels*
> *which had the seven vials full of the seven last*

plagues, and talked with me, saying, Come hither, I will show thee the bride, the Lamb's wife.

And he carried me away in the spirit to a great and high mountain, and showed me that great city, the holy Jerusalem, descending out of heaven from God,

Having the glory of God: and her light was like unto a stone most precious, even like a jasper stone, clear as crystal;

And had a wall great and high, and had twelve gates, and at the gates twelve angels, and names written thereon, which are the names of the twelve tribes of the children of Israel:

On the east three gates; on the north three gates; on the south three gates; and on the west three gates.

And the wall of the city had twelve foundations, and in them the names of the twelve apostles of the Lamb. (Rev. 21:9–14)

And the building of the wall of it was of jasper: and the city was pure gold, like unto clear glass.

And the foundations of the wall of the city were garnished with all manner of precious stones. The first foundation was jasper; the second, sapphire; the third, a chalcedony; the fourth, an emerald;

The fifth, sardonyx; the sixth, sardius, the seventh, chrysolyte; the eighth, beryl; the ninth, a topaz; the tenth, a chrysoprasus; the eleventh, a jacinth; the twelfth, an amethyst.

And the twelve gates were twelve pearls; and the street of the city was pure gold, as it were transparent glass.

*And I saw no temple therein: for the Lord God
Almighty and the Lamb are the temple of it.* (Rev.
21:18–22)

To understand the foundation of the wall and the gates, we
have to go to the Old Testament. There are no actual walls and
gates, but God Himself and Jesus Christ and His glory.

*Violence shall no more be heard in thy land,
wasting nor destruction within thy borders; but
thou shalt call thy walls Salvation, and thy gates
Praise.* (Isa. 60:18)

*And said unto him, Run, speak to this young man,
saying, Jerusalem shall be inhabited as towns without
walls for the multitude of men and cattle therein:*
    *For I, saith the Lord, will be unto her a wall of
fire round about, and will be the glory in the midst
of her.* (Zech. 2:4–5)

God said He would be the glory in the midst of her. The glory
in the form of a cloud can be seen during worship in the Old
Testament. Today, those who can see in the spirit will tell you that
they see the glory cloud during worship.

Jesus tells us that He is the door, the gate.

*Verily, verily, I say unto you, He that entereth not
by the door into the sheepfold, but climbeth up
some other way, the same is a thief and a robber.*
    *But he that entereth in by the door is the
shepherd of the sheep.*
    *To him the porter openeth; and the sheep hear
His voice: and He calleth His sheep by name, and
leadeth them out.*

> *And when He putteth forth his own sheep, He goeth before them, and the sheep follow Him: for they know His voice.*
>
> *And a stranger will they not follow, but will flee from him: for they know not the voice of strangers.*
>
> *This parable spake Jesus unto them: but they understood not what things they were which He spake unto them.*
>
> *Then said Jesus unto them again, Verily, verily, I say unto you, I am the door of the sheep.* (John 10:1–7)

The foundation is being able to hear the voice of God and obeying what He says. The wall is salvation, meaning covering and protection. The gate is praise.

Then how do we enter into it? David informs us in Psalm 100.

> *Make a joyful noise unto the Lord, all ye lands.*
>
> *Serve the Lord with gladness: come before His presence with singing.*
>
> *Know ye that the Lord He is God: it is He that hath made us, and not we ourselves; we are his people, and the sheep of His pasture.*
>
> *Enter into His gates with thanksgiving, and into His courts with praise: be thankful unto Him, and bless His name.*
>
> *For the Lord is good; His mercy is everlasting; and his truth endureth to all generations.* (Ps. 100:1–5)

Isaiah also gives us a clue when he says, "Thy borders [walls] Salvation, and thy gates Praise" (Isa. 60:18).

> *In that day shall this song be sung in the land of Judah; We have a strong city; salvation will God appoint for walls and bulwarks.*

*Open ye the gates, that the righteous nation
which keepeth the truth may enter in.* (Isa. 26:1–2)

Although the pattern of the tabernacle remains the same from Genesis to Revelation, it is the spiritual meaning behind each part of it that we should understand. Entering the gate remains the same.

David understands how to enter into the spiritual gate, which is activated by praise and worship in the natural, when he leads the people in worship after bringing the ark into the place prepared for it in the city of David.

When Solomon dedicates the temple, the glory of the Lord manifests in the form of a cloud. The singers and musicians come on one accord in pure worship, thanksgiving, and praise to God, after they have sanctified themselves (2 Chron. 5:12–14; 2 Chron. 6:1).

Heaven, the spiritual realm, is opened to Isaiah when he begins to worship with the angels, singing, "Holy, holy, holy, is the Lord of hosts: the whole earth is full of His glory" (Isa. 6:3).

It doesn't have to be singing and dancing; the gates will open in prayer. Notice Jesus teaching His disciples to pray; it always begins with praise: "And He said unto them, When ye pray, say, Our Father, which art in heaven, Hallowed be thy name. Thy kingdom come. Thy will be done, as in heaven, so in earth" (Luke 11:2).

We don't want to enter in and stop at the gate; our purpose for going in is to enter into God's very presence. Opening the gate is just the beginning.

At the gate a cloud will appear when the Lord hears. And, yes, God hears our praise and worship. Praise is what we do before we approach the burnt altar.

CHAPTER FOUR

THE ALTAR OF BURNT OFFERING

God commands Moses to make an altar of earth or of stone.

These were temporary altars as the children of Israel went from place to place before the tabernacle was built. We see Abraham and Jacob build these temporary altars as they travel in the Promised Land. Elijah also builds an altar of stone on Mt. Carmel.

> *And the Lord said unto Moses, Thus thou shalt say unto the children of Israel, Ye have seen that I have talked with you from heaven.*
>
> *Ye shall not make with me gods of silver, neither shall ye make unto you gods of gold.*
>
> *And altar of earth thou shalt make unto me, and shalt sacrifice thereon thy burnt offerings, and thy peace offerings, thy sheep, and thine oxen: in all places where I record my name I will come unto thee, and I will bless thee.*
>
> *And it thou wilt make me an altar of stone, thou shalt not build it of hewn stone: for if thou lift up thy tool upon it, thou hast polluted it.*

> *Neither shalt thou go up by steps unto mine altar, that thy nakedness be not discovered thereon.* (Exod. 20:22–26)

> *And Elijah said unto the people, Come near unto me. And all the people came near unto him. And he repaired the altar of the Lord that was broken down.*
>
> *And Elijah took twelve stones, according to the number of the tribes of the sons of Jacob, unto whom the word of the Lord came, saying, Israel shall be thy name:*
>
> *And with the stones he built an altar in the name of the Lord: and he made a trench about the altar, as great as would contain two measures of seed.* (1 Kings 18:30–32)

Note that the scripture says the altar has been broken down! What does that mean? For this is after the temple of Solomon had been built.

The temple has not been broken down, but the relationship between God and the children of Israel has been broken. The ten tribes of Israel, under the leadership of Ahab, are worshipping the two golden calves in Dan and Bethel that king Jeroboam made generations before. He made them to prevent the children of Israel under his leadership from returning to Jerusalem and the house of David (his grandson Rehoboam) during the feast. They are worshipping idols; the very thing God commanded them not to do.

God commands Moses to build a portable tabernacle, a place of worship that contains the vessels thereof as well as the burnt altar.

> *And thou shalt make an altar of shittim would, five cubits long, and five cubits broad; the altar*

shall be foursquare: and the height thereof shall be three cubits.

And thou shalt make the horns of it upon the four corners thereof: his horns shall be of the same: and thou shalt overlay it with brass.

And thou shalt make his pans to receive his ashes, and his shovels, and his basins, and his fleshhooks, and his firepans: all the vessels there of thou shalt make of brass.

And thou shalt make for it a grate of network of brass; and upon the net shalt thou make four brazen rings in the four corners thereof.

And thou shalt put it under the compass of the altar beneath, that the net may be even to the midst of the altar.

And thou shalt make staves for the altar, staves of shittim wood, and overlay them with brass.

And the staves shall be put into the rings, and the staves shall be upon the two sides of the altar, to bear it.

Hollow with boards shalt thou make it: as it was showed thee in the mount, so shall they make it. (Exod. 27:1–8)

THE PURPOSE OF THE BURNT ALTAR

God is very specific because every part of the burnt altar and its vessels has a spiritual meaning. For instance, the sides of the altar have four rings in them, two on each side. It also has staves that are placed in the rings when the altar is being transported. The priests—the sons of Kohath, the son of Levi—are responsible for carrying the altar on their shoulders. This act of carrying the altar represents the responsibility of the priests in knowing and understanding the part of the offeror in offering sacrifices, as well as knowing his own responsibilities during the sacrifice.

The brazen altar, sometimes called the burnt altar, is the place the children of Israel come to offer their sacrifices unto God to be cleansed and making their vows to God.

When the offeror first comes to the altar, he has to tell the priest why he wants to offer his sacrifice. Without knowing why he has come, the priest will not know what part of the animal goes on the altar, nor will he know what to do with the blood of the animal.

In the tabernacle of Moses and in the temple of Solomon, when an offeror came before the priests, the priest had to first check the offering to make sure it was without blemish. If it was blemished, he could not accept the sacrifice. But if it was without blemish, the priest handed it back to the offeror, placing it under his left arm. Then the priest picked up the basin and gave the offeror a sharp knife to cut the throat of the sacrifice. The priest then caught the blood of the animal in the basin. After the blood had drained out the animal, it was handed to the priests to flay and cut the animal up in a certain manner before washing it. The reason the offeror came to sacrifice determined where the blood was sprinkled, what part of the animal actually went on the burnt altar to present to God; it also determined whether the priest was to receive a part, which part he received, and whether the priest ate his portion in the temple or could take it home to share with his family.

Under the new and living way, the priests are responsible for informing the offeror the proper manner of offering his sacrifice, just as in the instructions given to Moses. For instance, when a person wants to accept Jesus Christ as their Lord and Savior, it is the responsibility of the minister to tell the offeror what to confess. Or if a man and woman stand before the altar to be married, it is the responsibility of the priest or minister to tell the couple what vows to confess. To confess means to speak aloud. God will not accept the sacrifice unless it is spoken.

The confession, the words spoken at the altar, becomes the sacrifice: the sacrifice of your lips. These are not just the words of the offeror but the priest's words also. They can't be just any words, but must be the words God requires.

For instance,, after the man and woman have said their vows, it becomes the responsibility of the priest or minister to pray to God for them and then pronounce them husband and wife. And when a person has confessed Jesus Christ as Lord and Savior, it becomes the responsibility of the priest or minister to pray to God for him or her and to pronounce them as Christian.

> *O Israel, return unto the Lord thy God; for thou hast fallen by thine iniquity.*
> *Take with you words, and turn to the Lord: say unto Him, Take away all iniquity, and receive us graciously: so will we render the calves of our lips.*
> (Hosea 14:1–2)

Every time we offer a sacrifice at the burnt altar, in sincerity, no matter the reason, God considers it a praise unto Him, a sacrifice of praise: "By Him therefore let us offer the sacrifice of praise to God continually, that is, the fruit of our lips giving thanks to His name" (Heb. 13:15; Josh. 7:19).

TYPES OF SACRIFICES OFFERED ON THE BURNT ALTAR

God gives the commandment of the five main sacrifices to Moses, and he instructs the children of Israel. They are listed in detail and with specific instructions. If you don't pay attention, it will seem as if He is saying the same thing over again with each sacrifice, but in each chapter the instructions are different—some slightly and some completely. It is not the animal that makes the difference, but the purpose of the sacrifice. What the offeror can afford determines what animal he brings to sacrifice.

There are two things God requires of each sacrifice: that the offeror come at his own voluntary will and that the sacrifice be without blemish. He cannot be forced, frightened, or coerced to bring an offering. If the sacrifice has any blemishes whatsoever, the priests are instructed not to receive it and turn the offeror away. It they receive it, according to the first and second books of Malachi, the priests will be cursed by God.

Let us look at the different sacrifices listed in Leviticus.

THE WHOLE BURNT OFFERING:

The blood was sprinkled round about the about the altar. The entire animal is flayed into pieces; the innards and legs are washed and then placed on the altar to be burned.

This sacrifice represents the vow of consecration of a man's or woman's whole heart to the Lord God. Today it is the giving one's heart to Jesus Christ and asking Him to be their Lord and Savior: "And thou shalt love the Lord thy God with all thy heart, and with all thy soul, and with all thy mind, and with all thy strength: this is the first commandment" (Mark 12:30).

THE PEACE OFFERING:

The animal is flayed into pieces, but only the fat that covered the innards, the kidneys, the caul, and the liver are placed on the burnt altar to be burned and offered to God. The so-called wave breast and heave shoulder are given to the priests to wave before the Lord; these are permitted to be taken home and shared with their family. The blood of the animal is sprinkled about the altar.

This sacrifice represents the vow of thanksgiving and praise to God in everything we do and say.

> *They that observe lying vanities forsake their own*
> *mercy.*
>   *But I will sacrifice unto thee with the voice of*
> *thanksgiving; I will pay that that I have vowed.*
> (Jon. 2:8–9)

> *Giving thanks always for all things unto God and*
> *the Father in the name of our Lord Jesus Christ.*
> (Eph. 5:20)

THE SIN OFFERING:

The animal is flayed into pieces; the fat that covered the innards, the kidneys, the caul, and the liver are placed on the burnt altar to be burned and offered to God. The wave breast and the heave shoulder are given to the priests to be eaten in the tabernacle, and the rest of the animal is carried outside the camp to a clean place and burned.

The blood of the animal is taken inside the Holy Place; the priest dips his finger in the blood and then sprinkles the blood seven times before the veil of the sanctuary. Some of the blood is placed on the horns of the altar of incense; the rest of the blood is poured out at the bottom of the altar of burnt offering.

This offering represents the confession and renouncing of the offeror's sins; asking for mercy (forgiveness), whether the misdeed was intentional or unintentional; forgiving others; apologizing for offending others; and cleansing from defilement. One of the biggest problems Christians have is forgiving others. This too must be confessed, with the confessor specifically calling each person by name.

If my people, which are called by my name, shall humble themselves, and pray, and seek my face, and turn from their wicked ways; then will I hear from heaven, and will forgive their sin, and will heal their land. (2 Chron. 7:14)

Therefore if thou bring thy gift to the altar, and there rememberest that thy brother hath aught against thee;

Leave there thy gift before the altar, and go thy way; first be reconciled to thy brother, and then come and offer thy gift.

Agree with thine adversary quickly, whiles thou art in the way with him; lest at any time the adversary deliver thee to the judge, and the judge deliver thee to the officer, and thou be cast into prison.

Verily I say unto thee, Thou shalt by no means come out thence, till thou hast paid the uttermost farthing. (Matt. 5:23–26)

And when ye stand praying, forgive, if ye have aught against any: that your Father also which is in heaven may forgive you your trespasses.

But if ye do not forgive, neither will your Father which is in heaven forgive your trespasses. (Mark 11:25–26)

THE TRESPASS OFFERING:

A trespass is a sin against man and or holy things of God, such as overhearing swearing and keeping silent, stealing, touching any unclean thing, or sinning ignorantly in the things of the

Lord. Beyond asking for mercy, some restitution is required. The trespass offering is not only a confession and vow, but also an action of returning what is stolen with interest.

The trespass offering represents the confession of the sin, asking for forgiveness, and making restitution.

> *And David's anger was greatly kindled against the*
> *man; and he said to Nathan, As the Lord liveth,*
> *the man that hath done this thing shall surely die:*
> *And he shall restore the lamb fourfold, because*
> *he did this thing, and because he had no pity.* (2
> Sam. 12:5–6)

Nathan informs David that he, David, was the man who had stolen another man's sheep (2 Sam. 12:7).

God, speaking through Nathan, says that because he has done this thing, the sword will never depart from his house, and his wives will be given to another man, and that the other man will lie with them in the sight of the sun.

David repents, and God forgives him, but even the child that has been born to Bathsheba dies (2 Sam. 12:11–14).

Because of David's sin of taking another man's wife, and then having the man killed, David's son Amon rapes his own sister; his son Absalom kills his half brother Amon for raping his sister; and later Absalom tries to take the throne from David. David's son Adonijah later tries to take the throne and marry Abishag the Shunammite, the concubine of David, which would signify that he was king. Because of that, Solomon has Adonijah killed. Because of David's trespass, four of his sons die or are killed, and Solomon marries strange wives who lead him into idolatry.

In the New Testament Zacchaeus offers his trespass offering.

> *And Zacchaeus stood, and said unto the Lord:*
> *Behold, Lord, the half of my goods I give to the*

> poor; and if I have taken any thing from any man
> by false accusation, I restore him fourfold.
>   And Jesus said unto him, This day is salvation
> come to this house, forsomuch as he also is a son of
> Abraham. (Luke 19:8–9)

Leviticus 5 informs us that we are to confess a sin in which we overheard someone else swearing or blaspheming, or if they pronounced with the lips an oath to do evil.

The hearer has to place his right hand on the head of the one who swore, transferring the sin from himself back to the one who said it before stoning him to death along with the congregation.

Today we simply confess to God what we have heard and ask Him to forgive us.

THE MEAT (MEAL) OFFERING:

The meat offering actually has no meat in it and is to be offered with each of the other animal sacrifices along with the drink offering.

The meat offering is to be fine flour, oil, frankincense, and salt. If the offeror does not have fine flour, barley can be used. It can be offered as grain, baked cakes, wafers, or fried in a pan. The priest only takes a memorial of the offering to be placed on the altar with the animal sacrifice. No leaven or honey is to be burned with the meat offering. Every meat offering has to be seasoned with salt.

The meat offering represents the manna eaten in the wilderness, the word of God, the body of Jesus, and the bread of communion. It also represents the labor that went into raising the grain, harvesting it, winnowing it, grinding it, and cooking it.

The meat offering represents a vow of consecration of your time every day (in prayer and study of God's word) in covenant.

At Galeed, Jacob makes a covenant with his father-in-law

Laban. He gathers stones and makes a pillar as witness of the covenant. Then he offers sacrifice on the mount and calls his brethren to eat bread as a testimony (Gen. 31:43–55).

> *For I have received of the Lord that which also I delivered unto you, That the Lord Jesus the same night in which He was betrayed took bread:*
>
> *And when He had given thanks, He broke it, and said, Take, eat: this is my body, which is broken for you: this do in remembrance of me.*
>
> *After the same manner also He took the cup, when He had supped, saying, This cup is the New Testament in my blood: this do ye, as often as ye drink it, in remembrance of me.*
>
> *For as often as ye eat this bread, and drink this cup, ye do show the Lord's death till He come.* (1 Cor. 11:23–26)

> *I am that bread of life.*
>
> *Your fathers did eat manna in the wilderness, and are dead.*
>
> *This is the bread which cometh down from heaven, that a man may eat thereof, and not die.*
>
> *I am the living bread which came down from heaven: if any man eat of this bread, he shall live forever: and the bread that I will give is my flesh, which I will give for the life of the world.* (John 6:48–51)

THE DRINK OFFERING:

According to the law of Moses, a drink offering is to be presented along with the burnt offerings and the meat offering (Exodus 29:40; Leviticus 23:13; Numbers 15:1-10).

Both the olive and grape have to be crushed to extract the liquid within. Jesus experiences this crushing: being humiliated and beaten by the soldiers, made naked and nailed on the cross, feeling the rejection of the people and the priests, and being pierced in the side.

The drink offering represents the crushing of His Spirit and the shedding of His blood that we might be filled with that which He shed, His Holy Spirit (John 19:34; Acts 2:33; Titus 3:5–6).

In partaking in the drink offering through communion, you are renewing the vow you made of complete obedience and willingness to God, no matter what it costs. You are also asking the Lord to refill you with His Holy Spirit, the seal of your salvation.

> *Then Jesus said unto them, Verily, verily, I say unto you, Except ye eat the flesh of the Son of man, and drink His blood, ye have no life in you.*
>
> *Whoso eateth my flesh, and drinketh my blood, hath eternal life; and I will raise him up at the last day.* (John 6:53–54)

THE SALT OFFERING:

Every meat offering is seasoned with salt. Salt is an antiseptic and a preventive of putrefaction (decay) and is used for its preserving qualities.

Leviticus 2:13 says, "And every oblation of thy meat offering shalt thou season with salt; neither shalt thou suffer the salt of the covenant of thy God to be lacking from thy meat offering: with all thine offerings thou shalt offer salt." Salt is used as an unbreakable sign of the covenant between man and God.

The salt offering represents the vow of an unbreakable eternal agreement between God and man.

> *All the heave offerings of the holy things, which the children of Israel offer unto the Lord, have I given thee, and thy sons and thy daughters with thee, by a statute for ever: it is a covenant of salt forever before the Lord unto thee and to thy seed with thee.* (Num. 18:19)

> *Ought ye not to know that the Lord God of Israel gave the kingdom of Israel to David for ever, even to him and to his sons by a covenant of salt?* (2 Chron. 13:5)

Because Jesus died on the cross and became the Lamb of God, we are no longer required to bring an animal sacrifice, but we offer the sacrifice of our lips. The priests and prophets in the Old Testament understood this; that is why you will note that when certain prophets—Moses, Daniel, sometimes David—offer sacrifice, they do not build a physical altar when they pray.

> *I acknowledge my sin unto thee, and mine iniquity have I not hid. I said, I will confess my transgression unto the Lord; and thou forgavest the iniquity of my sin. Selah.* (Ps. 32:5)

> *Now when Daniel knew that the writing was signed, he went into his house; and his windows being open in his chamber toward Jerusalem, he kneeled upon his knees three times a day, and prayed, and gave thanks before his God, as he did aforetime.* (Dan. 6:10)

> *If we confess our sins, He is faithful and just to forgive us our sins, and to cleanse us from all unrighteousness.* (1 John 1:9)

The sacrifice has to be from your heart, and it has to mean something to you.

> *And it came to pass after these things, that God did tempt Abraham, and said unto him, Abraham: and he said, Behold, here I am.*
>
> *And He said, Take now thy son, thine only son Isaac, whom thou lovest, and get thee into the land of Moriah; and offer him there for a burnt offering upon one of the mountains which I will tell thee of.* (Gen. 22:1–2)

God required Abraham to offer that which he loved the most; his sacrifice had to be from his heart.

> *Speak ye unto all the congregation of Israel, saying, In the tenth day of this month they shall take to them every man a lamb, according to the house of their fathers, a lamb for a house.*
>
> *And if the household be too little for the lamb, let him and his neighbor next unto his house take it according to the number of the souls; every man according to his eating shall make your count for the lamb.*
>
> *Your lamb shall be without blemish, a male of the first year: ye shall take it out from the sheep, or from the goats:*
>
> *And ye shall keep it up until the fourteenth day of the same month: and the whole assembly of the congregation of Israel shall kill it in the evening.* (Exod. 12:3–6)

Keeping a young animal next to the entrance of the house would cause the entire family to fall in love with the animal. It was

God's plan that they offered something that they loved, something from the heart.

> *Examine me, O Lord, and prove me; try my reins*
> *and my heart.* (Ps. 26:2)

David understood this fact and stated it often in his writing.

The kidney or reins refers to the mind, the will and the intellect (H3620 in *The Exhaustive Concordance of the Bible* by James Strong).

Liver or loins, being in the area between the lowest part of the rib and the hip bone, bowels refers to the heart; the seat of one's emotions (H3516 in Strong's *Concordance*).

The New Testament references the giving of the whole heart to God:

> *And thou shalt love the Lord thy God with all*
> *thy heart, and with all thy soul, and with all thy*
> *mind, and with all thy strength: this is the first*
> *commandment.* (Mark 12:30)

The fat about the kidney, liver, caul, and sometimes the rump represents the strength, the ability in which the offeror comes before God in humility, brokenness, and sincerity.

> *The sacrifices of God are a broken spirit: a broken*
> *and a contrite heart, O God, thou wilt not despise.*
> (Ps. 51:17)

> *For thus saith the high and lofty One that*
> *inhabiteth eternity, whose name is Holy; I dwell in*
> *the high and Holy Place, with him also that is of a*
> *contrite and humble spirit, to revive the spirit of*

> *the humble, and to revive the heart of the contrite*
> *ones.* (Isa. 57:15)

God will not minister to those who will not humble themselves before Him. Jesus was not anointed to minister to those who did not believe and those who were prideful.

> *The Spirit of the Lord God is upon me; because*
> *the Lord hath anointed me to preach good tidings*
> *unto the meek; He hath sent me to bind up the*
> *brokenhearted, to proclaim liberty to the captives,*
> *and the opening of the prison to them that are*
> *bound.* (Isa. 61:1)

> *Blessed are the poor in spirit: for theirs is the*
> *kingdom of heaven.* (Matt. 5:3)

Understand, once Jesus becomes a minister, the burnt altar becomes portable again. Every place a minister of the gospel goes, he takes the burnt altar with him. It didn't matter whether Jesus is on the side of a mountain, on a ship, in the temple, the synagogue, or in someone's house; He ministered as a priest in the temple.

> *What? Know ye not that your body is the temple*
> *of the Holy Ghost which is in you, which ye have of*
> *God, and ye are not your own?* (1 Cor. 6:19)

CHAPTER FIVE

THE BRAZEN LAVER

In Exodus, God commands Moses to make a brazen laver and place it in the court of the tabernacle and of the temple along with the burnt altar. The laver is a large basin that contains water for cleansing the hands and feet of the priest before he enters into the Holy Place.

> *And the Lord spake unto Moses, saying,*
>
> *Thou shalt also make a laver of brass, and his foot also of brass, to wash withal: and thou shalt put it between the tabernacle of the congregation and the altar, and thou shalt put water therein.*
>
> *For Aaron and his sons shall wash their hands and their feet thereat:*
>
> *When they go into the tabernacle of the congregation, they shall wash with water, that they die not; or when they come near to the altar to minister, to burn offering made of fire unto the Lord:*
>
> *So they shall wash their hands and their feet, that they die not: and it shall be a statute forever to them, even to him and to his seed throughout their generations.* (Exod. 30:17–21)

> *And he made the laver of brass, and the foot of*
> *it of brass, of the looking glasses of the women*
> *assembling, which assembled at the door of the*
> *tabernacle of the congregation.* (Exod. 38:8)

In the day of Moses, people did not use glass as mirrors as we do today. They used pieces of metal. If you take a polished bowl-shaped piece of metal—whether brass, silver, or gold—and fill it with water, when you look inside, the shape of the bowl will cause the water to act as a mirror.

The brazen laver acted as a mirror for the priests when they went to wash themselves after having caught the blood of the animal that had been sacrificed. If a priest entered the Holy Place with the blood on his person, being unclean, he would die as he entered.

The brazen laver reminds the priest to sanctify himself before he enters the Holy Place to go before the altar of incense to intercede for the offeror. The offeror lays his hands on the head of the sacrifice to transfer his sins from himself to the animal. The blood of the animal is considered unclean; it splatters on the hands and feet of the priest, which makes him unclean. Simply hearing the confession of the offeror causes the priest to be unclean, leading him to need to sanctify himself before entering into the Holy Place.

In Leviticus 24, two young men hear another young man blaspheme God, and they go and tell Moses. Moses goes to God to find out what to do. God requires the two young men to lay their hands on the head of the one who blasphemed, transferring the sin back to him. Then the rest of the congregation stone him to death.

> *And the Israelitish woman's son blasphemed the*
> *name of the Lord, and cursed. And they brought him*
> *unto Moses: (and his mother's name was Shelomith,*
> *the daughter of Dibri, of the tribe of Dan:)*

*And they put him in ward, that the mind of the
Lord might be showed them.*

And the Lord spake unto Moses, saying,

*Bring forth him that hath cursed without the
camp; and let all that heard him lay their hands
upon his head, and let all the congregation stone
him.* (Lev. 24:11–14)

It is the responsibility of the priests to understand the purpose
of the brazen laver. It too was carried upon the shoulders of the
priests as they traveled. When we compare the laver of Moses to
that of Solomon, we see that the latter was very pointed about this
responsibility.

*Moreover he made an altar of brass, twenty cubits
the length thereof, and twenty cubits the breadth
thereof, and ten cubits the height thereof.*

*Also he made a molten sea of ten cubits from
brim to brim, round in compass, and five cubits
the height thereof; and a line of thirty cubits did
compass it round about.*

*And under it was the similitude of oxen,
which did compass it round about: ten in cubit,
compassing the sea round about. Two rows of oxen
were cast, when it was cast.*

*It stood upon twelve oxen, three looking toward
the north, and three looking toward the west, and
three looking toward the south, and three looking
toward the east: and the sea was set above upon
them, and all their hinder parts were inward.*

*And the thickness of it was a handbreadth, and
the brim of it like the work of the brim of a cup,
with flowers of lilies; and it received and held three
thousand baths.*

> *He made also ten lavers, and put five on the right hand, and five on the left, to wash in them: such things as they offered for the burnt offering they washed in them; but the sea was for the priests to wash in. (2 Chron. 4:1–6)*

The brazen laver God commanded Moses to make was to be carried upon the shoulders of the priests, but the brazen laver Solomon made was set upon the shoulders of the twelve oxen. An ox represents a priest or minister of the gospel. Solomon's laver had twelve oxen, representing the twelve tribes of Israel.

> *For it is written in the law of Moses, Thou shalt not muzzle the mouth of the ox that treadeth out the corn. Doth God take care for oxen?*
> *Or saith He it altogether for our sakes? For our sakes, no doubt, this is written: that he that ploweth should plow in hope; and that he that thresheth in hope should be partaker of his hope. (1 Cor. 9:9–10)*

> *And Ephraim is as a heifer that is taught, and loveth to tread out the corn; but I passed over upon her fair neck: I will make Ephraim to ride; Judah shall plow, and Jacob shall break his clods. (Hos. 10:11)*

The "sea" of glass mingled with fire was seen by John the Revelator. God's word is water and it is fire—it cleanses your heart and your mind! The brazen altar and the brazen laver work hand in hand. John the Baptist states this in the book of Matthew: "I indeed baptize you with water unto repentance: but He that cometh after me is mightier than I, whose shoes I am not worthy to bear: He shall baptize you with the Holy Ghost, and with fire" (Matt. 3:11).

And before the throne there was a sea of glass like unto crystal: and in the midst of the throne, and round about the throne, were four beasts full of eyes before and behind. (Rev. 4:6)

And I saw as it were a sea of glass mingled with fire: and them that had gotten the victory over the beast, and over his image, and over his mark, and over the number of his name, stand on the sea of glass, having the harps of God. (Rev. 15:2)

The laver contained the water that washes away sin. Cleansing in the brazen laver can be seen in baptism, in the water of purification of the red heifer. Just as the priests washed at the brazen laver, for the same purpose the children of Israel crossed the Red Sea, the Jordan River, and in the New Testament Christians are baptized. This all stressed the importance of holiness.

And a man that is clean shall gather up the ashes of the heifer, and lay them up without the camp in a clean place, and it shall be kept for the congregation of the children of Israel for a water of separation: it is a purification for sin. (Num. 19:9)

And for an unclean person they shall take of the ashes of the burnt heifer of purification for sin, and running water shall be put thereto in a vessel:
And a clean person shall take hyssop, and dip it in the water, and sprinkle it upon the tent, and upon all the vessels, and upon the persons that were there, and upon him that touched a bone, or one slain, or one dead, or a grave:
And the clean person shall sprinkle upon the unclean on the third day, and on the seventh day:

and on the seventh day he shall purify himself, and wash his clothes, and bathe himself in water, and shall be clean at even. (Num. 19:17–19)

John did baptize in the wilderness, and preach the baptism of repentance for the remission of sins.

And there went out unto him all the land of Judea, and they of Jerusalem, and were all baptized of him in the river Jordan, confessing their sins (Mark 1:4–5)

Moreover, brethren, I would not that ye should be ignorant, how that all our fathers were under the cloud, and all passed through the sea;

And were all baptized unto Moses in the cloud and in the sea;

And did all eat the same spiritual meat;

And did all drink the same spiritual drink: for they drank of that spiritual Rock that followed them: and that Rock was Christ. (1 Cor. 10:1–4)

Know ye not, that so many of us as were baptized into Jesus Christ were baptized into His death?

Therefore we are buried with Him by baptism into death: that like as Christ was raised up from the dead by the glory of the Father, even so we also should walk in newness of life.

For if we have been planted together in the likeness of His death, we shall be also in the likeness of His resurrection:

Knowing this, that our old man is crucified with Him, that the body of sin might be destroyed, that henceforth we should not serve sin.

For he that is dead is freed from sin. (Rom. 6:3–7)

> *Jesus answered, Verily, verily, I say unto thee,*
> *Except a man be born of water and of the Spirit,*
> *he cannot enter the kingdom of God.* (John 3:5)

In the Gospels, we see how one man's sin contaminates others when Judas betrays Jesus. The disciples and Jesus have eaten a meal together when Judas steps out to betray Him. No, the disciples do not know what he is doing, but the mere fact that he has just shared fellowship and bread with them causes all the disciples to be a part of his actions.

> *He riseth from supper, and laid aside His garments;*
> *and took a towel, and girded Himself.*
> *After that He poureth water into a basin, and*
> *began to wash the disciples' feet, and to wipe them*
> *with the towel wherewith He was girded.*
> *Then cometh he to Simon Peter: and Peter saith*
> *unto Him, Lord, dost thou wash my feet?*
> *Jesus answered and said unto him, What I*
> *do thou knowest not now; but thou shalt know*
> *hereafter.* (John 13:4–7)

While the burnt altar burns up the sin, the brazen laver cleanses the residue of sin away. As it says in 1 John 1, when we confess the sin, God forgives us, but there still has to be a cleansing. Also, in Exodus 33, Moses breaks the golden calf and burns it, then throws the ashes into the water.

Even though the sin has been forgiven, there may still be a lingering sign that the sin had been present, even the dust on your feet.

For instance, you may have repented and renounced your participation in an organization, but you still have the special clothing you wore at your dedication to that organization. You may have married, but you still have photos or gifts from the person in a past relationship. You may have given your life to Jesus Christ, but you still have books of horror, the occult, or pornography in your home. These things give an unclean spirit the right to remain.

> *And many that believed came, and confessed, and showed their deeds.*
>
> *Many of them also which used curious arts brought their books together, and burned them before all men: and they counted the price of them, and found it fifty thousand pieces of silver.* (Acts 19:18–19)

> *Having therefore, brethren, boldness to enter into the holiest by the blood of Jesus,*
>
> *By a new and living way, which He hath consecrated for us, through the veil, that is to say, his flesh;*
>
> *And having a high priest over the house of God;*
>
> *Let us draw near with a true heart in full assurance of faith, having our hearts sprinkled from an evil conscience, and our bodies washed with pure water.* (Heb. 10:19–22)

CHAPTER SIX

THE GOLDEN CANDLESTICK

We leave the court of the tabernacle, where the unclean may enter; and we enter through the veil into the Holy Place, in which only those who are holy may enter.

Only the priests could go through the veil into the Holy Place to seek wisdom, understanding, and intercede for the people. Only the high priest ministered at the golden candlestick and the golden table of showbread, making sure the candlestick was lit, refilling it with oil, placing fresh bread on the table each Sabbath, and placing fresh incense on the altar.

Only the sons of the high priests entered into the Holy Place and into the Holy of Holies to prepare the vessels for transportation as the children of Israel traveled. They were responsible for setting the vessels in place inside the tabernacle when the people camped.

God commanded Moses to make the candlestick.

> *And thou shalt make a candlestick of pure gold: of beaten work shall the candlestick be made: his shaft, and his branches, his bowls, his knops, and his flowers, shall be of the same.*
>
> *And six branches shall come out of the sides of it; three branches of the candlestick out of the one*

side, and three branches of the candlestick out of the other side.

Three bowls made like unto almonds, with a knop and a flower in one branch; and three bowls made like almonds in the other branch, with a knop and a flower; so in the six branches that come out of the candlestick.

And in the candlestick shall be four bowls made like unto almonds, with their knops and their flowers.

And there shall be a knop under two branches of the same, and a knop under two branches of the same, and a knop under two branches of the same, according to the six branches that proceed out of the candlestick.

Their knops and their branches shall be of the same: all it shall be one beaten work of pure gold.

And thou shalt make the seven lamps thereof: and they shall light the lamps thereof, that they may give light over against it.

And the tongs thereof, and the censers thereof, shall be of pure gold,

Of a talent of pure gold shall he make it, with all these vessels.

And look that thou make them after their pattern, which was showed thee in the mount. (Exod. 25:31–40)

And thou shalt set the table without the veil, and the candlestick over against the table on the side of the tabernacle toward the south: and thou shalt put the table on the north side. (Exod. 26:35)

The candlestick represents the Holy Spirit. Without the light of the candlestick, the Holy Place is completely dark.

Without the light of the candlestick, one would not know how to find the shewbread or the veil that opens into the Holy Place, the very presence of God. Without the light of the candlestick, everything in the Holy Place would be hidden from those who entered.

Without the Holy Spirit, no man can receive revelation and understanding of God's word, which the shewbread represents.

If the high priest was disobedient to God, the light went out. If a pastor of a church is walking in disobedience to God, the Holy Spirit will leave. Thus, there will be no new revelations from God, and there will be some form of chastisement to him and the congregation.

> *And the child Samuel ministered unto the Lord before Eli. And the word of the Lord was precious in those days; there was no open vision.*
>
> *And it came to pass at that time, when Eli was laid down in his place, and his eyes began to wax dim, that he could not see;*
>
> *And ere the lamp of God went out in the temple of the Lord, where the ark of God was, and Samuel was laid down to sleep.* (1 Sam. 3:1–3)

Notice that the candlestick was made with pure beaten gold. To refine gold the refiner had to heat it to a certain temperature until it became a liquid, then skim the impurities off the top. The process was repeated until the refiner had removed all of the impurities, and he could look into the melted gold and see himself clearly.

The Holy Spirit, the very Spirit of God, comes to dwell in those who have confessed their sins, given their lives to Jesus Christ, and invited Him in. He will not dwell in an unclean vessel. And according to Luke 11, we simply ask our heavenly Father for Him to come in.

He comes to be our Comforter, our Teacher, our Revealer of truth, our Reprover, our Guide, and Revealer of those things God is doing and of things to come. Jesus says in Matthew 5 that we become the light of the world. Each of us must be refined in the fire of God's word to purge away the dross of our hearts that we may be vessels worthy to contain the anointing of God. It is through afflictions that we are tried and purified.

> *And when they had preached the gospel to that city, and had taught many, they returned again to Lystra, and to Iconium, and Antioch,*
> *Confirming the souls of the disciples, and exhorting them to continue in the faith, and that we must through much tribulation enter into the kingdom of God.* (Acts 14:21–22)

> *Blessed is the man that endureth temptation: for when he is tried, he shall receive the crown of life, which the Lord hath promised to them that love Him.* (James 1:12)

> *Behold, I have refined thee, but not with silver; I have chosen thee in the furnace of affliction.* (Isa. 48:10)

The priests were responsible for making sure the candlestick was lighted always; therefore, the oil was never to go completely out. The oil came from olives that had been beaten and stepped on until crushed. If the light of the candlestick went out, it revealed that the priests had forsaken the Lord.

> *And thou shalt command the children of Israel, that they bring thee pure oil olive beaten for the light, to cause the lamp to burn always.*

> *In the tabernacle of the congregation without the veil, which is before the testimony, Aaron and his sons shall order it from evening to morning before the Lord: it shall be a statute for ever unto their generations on the behalf of the children of Israel.* (Exod. 27:20–21)

> *And they burn unto the Lord every morning and every evening burnt sacrifices and sweet incense: the shewbread also set they in order upon the pure table; and the candlestick of gold with the lamps thereof, to burn every evening: for we keep the charge of the Lord our God; but ye have forsaken Him.* (2 Chron. 13:11)

> *Remember therefore from whence thou art fallen, and repent, and do the first works; or else I will come unto thee quickly, and will remove thy candlestick out of his place, except thou repent.* (Rev. 2:5)

A house may be connected to the power lines and have electrical wire throughout the house, light switches on the walls, and light bulbs in the sockets, but if there is no electrical current, the wires, light switches, and bulbs are useless. In the same manner, without oil, the candlestick is useless. That oil represents the anointing of God, the Holy Spirit.

Once the current is reconnected, you can turn on the lights in the house. In like manner, we must be refilled with Spirit of God daily (Eph. 5:18).

> *And I will give power unto my two witnesses, and they shall prophesy a thousand two hundred and threescore days, clothed in sackcloth.*

> *These are the two olive trees, and the two candlesticks standing before the God of the earth.*
>
> *And if any man will hurt them, fire proceedeth out of their mouth, and devoureth their enemies: and if any man will hurt them, he must in this manner be killed.*
>
> *These have power to shut heaven, that it rain not in the days of their prophecy: and have power over waters to turn them to blood, and to smite the earth with all plagues, as often as they will.* (Rev. 11:3–6)

The purpose of the candlestick is to give light, illumination, revelation, and understanding. The word of God is a spiritual book, and without the Holy Spirit dwelling in you, you cannot understand His word, nor His mysteries; it will be as a history book or a novel to you.

> *In Him was life; and the life was the light of men.*
>
> *And the light shineth in darkness: and the darkness comprehended it not.* (John 1:4–5)

CHAPTER SEVEN

THE TABLE OF SHEWBREAD

In Exodus, God commands Moses to make the table of shewbread and gives him specific instructions:

> *Thou shalt also make a table of shittim wood: two cubits shall be the length thereof, and a cubit the breath thereof, and a cubit and a half the height thereof.*
>
> *And thou shalt overlay it with pure gold, and make thereto a crown of gold round about.*
>
> *And thou shalt make unto it a border of an hand breadth round about, and thou shalt make a golden crown to the border thereof round about.*
>
> *And thou shalt make for it four rings of gold, and put the rings in the four corners that are on the four feet thereof.*
>
> *Over against the border shall the rings be for places of the staves to bear the table.*
>
> *And thou shalt make the staves of shittim wood, and overlay them with gold, that the table may be borne with them.*
>
> *And thou shalt make the dishes thereof, and spoons thereof, and covers thereof, and bowls*

> *thereof, to cover withal: of pure gold shalt thou make them.* (Exod. 25:23–29)

Shittim wood is from the acacia tree. Acacia wood is beautiful, light, and virtually indestructible; it represents Christ's being indestructible. It was used throughout the structural framework of the tent of meeting and in the tabernacle furniture. Poles made of acacia wood were used to transport tabernacle furniture: the ark of the covenant, the table of shewbread, the altar of incense, and the burnt altar.

In the beginning God commands Moses that these sacred vessels be carried on the shoulders of the priests, thus the poles on the sides of the furniture. Numbers 7 informs us that God allows all but the ark of the covenant to be transported on carts driven by oxen, after the elders of each tribe offered wagons and oxen to transport the vessels.

Although the vessels were not carried on the shoulders of the priests, the priests were still responsible for the transportation of them.

A minister of the gospel of God is required to know truth, to be pure and holy at all times, being the table on which the bread of God lies.

The shewbread is the word of God, Jesus Christ. A minister of the gospel is responsible for having the word of God within his or her heart and speaking the truth of God's word at all times. Every Sabbath, after fresh bread was placed on the table, the old shewbread was eaten by the priest.

> *And other of their brethren, of the sons of Kohathites, were over the shewbread, to prepare it every Sabbath.* (1 Chron. 9:32)

> *I am the bread of life.*
>
> *Your fathers did eat manna in the wilderness, and are dead.*
>
> *This is the bread which cometh down from heaven, that a man may eat thereof, and not die.*
>
> *I am the living bread which came down from heaven: if any man eat of this bread, he shall live forever: and the bread that I will give is my flesh, which I will give for the life of the world.* (John 6:48–51)

The vessels of the tabernacle are an example and shadow of the true tabernacle.

> *Who serve unto the example and shadow of heavenly things, as Moses was admonished of God when he was about to make the tabernacle: for, See, saith He, that thou make all things according to the pattern showed to thee in the mount.*
>
> *But now hath He obtained a more excellent ministry, by how much also He is the mediator of a better covenant, which was established upon better promises.* (Heb. 8:5–6)

> *For the law having a shadow of good things to come, and not the very image of the things, can never with those sacrifices which they offered year by year continually make the corners thereunto perfect.* (Heb. 10:1)

Notice how both the table of shewbread and the candlestick are located in the Holy Place, inside a dark area of the tabernacle. The shewbread is the word of God, but without the light of the candlestick that contains the holy oil and represents the Holy Spirit, there is no understanding of God's word.

Both the candlestick and the table of shewbread are containers, the candlestick containing the holy oil, the table of shewbread containing the shewbread. In turn, Jesus was a man filled with the Spirit of God and in which the word of God lay. Jesus is without sin, holy, and filled with the Spirit of God. Jesus is also the word of God; He fully understood the truth of God's word. He knew how to teach man to have that same relationship with our Father; He proclaimed the word of God in His preaching and teaching; He lived the word of God, setting an example for us; and He knew the mysteries of the word of God.

> *And I saw in the right hand of Him that sat on the throne a book written within and on the backside, sealed with seven seals.*
>
> *And I saw a strong angel proclaiming with a loud voice, Who is worthy to open the book, and to loose the seals thereof?*
>
> *And no man in heaven, nor in earth, neither under the earth, was able to open the book, neither to look thereon.*
>
> *And I wept much, because no man was found worthy to open and to read the book, neither to look thereon.*
>
> *And one of the elders saith unto me, Weep not: behold, the Lion of the tribe of Juda, the Root of David, hath prevailed to open the book, and to loose the seven seals thereof.*
>
> *And I beheld, and, lo, in the midst of the throne and of the four beasts, and in the midst of the elders, stood a Lamb as it had been slain, having seven horns and seven eyes, which are the seven Spirits of God sent forth into all the earth.*

*And He came and took the book out of the right
hand of Him that sat upon the throne.* (Rev. 5:1–7)

Jesus will give the light of the word to all those who seek Him
diligently.

In Him was life; and the life was the light of men.
(John 1:4)

*That was the true Light, which lighteth every man
that cometh into the world.* (John 1:9)

We then become witnesses of the Light and the word.

*Ye are the light of the world. A city that is set on a
hill cannot be hid.*
*Neither do men light a candle, and put it under
a bushel, but on a candlestick; and it giveth light
unto all that are in the house.*
*Let your light so shine before men, that they
may see your good works, and glorify your Father
which is in heaven.* (Matt. 5:14–16)

Believers become the light of the world, being filled with His
Spirit, and God's word. What Jesus did, we are to do also.

*And the voice which I heard from heaven spake
unto me again, and said, Go and take the little
book which is open in the hand of the angel which
standeth upon the sea and upon the earth.*
*And I went unto the angel, and said unto him,
Give me the little book, And he said unto me, Take
it, and eat it up; and it shall make thy belly bitter,
but it shall be in thy mouth sweet as honey.*

And I took the little book out of the angel's hand, and ate it up; and it was in my mouth sweet as honey: and as soon as I had eaten it, my belly was bitter.

And He said unto me, Thou must prophesy again before many peoples, and nations, and tongues, and kings. (Rev. 10:8–11)

CHAPTER EIGHT

THE ALTAR OF INCENSE

Incense is symbolic of smoke ascending up to God as a sweet smell. In the Bible it refers to the prayers. Likewise, the smoke of the burnt offering also represents prayers. Being that the smoke of the two of them were from different sources, the prayers are two different types of prayers.

Notice how specific God's instructions are for making the incense, the ingredients, and the location of this altar in the temple.

INSTRUCTIONS FOR MAKING THE ALTAR OF INCENSE

And thou shalt make an altar to burn incense upon: of shittim wood shalt thou make it.

A cubit shall be the length thereof, and a cubit the breadth thereof; four square shall it be: and two cubits shall be the height thereof: the horns thereof shall be of the same.

And thou shalt overlay it with pure gold, the top thereof, and the sides thereof round about, and the horns thereof; and thou shalt make unto it a crown of gold round about.

And two golden rings shalt thou make to it under the crown of it, by the two corners thereof, upon the two sides of it shalt thou make it; and they shall be for places for the staves to bear it withal.

And thou shalt make the staves of shittim wood, and overlay them with gold.

And thou shalt put it before the veil that is by the ark of the testimony, before the mercy seat that is over the testimony, where I will meet with thee.

And Aaron shall burn thereon sweet incense every morning: when he dresseth the lamps, he shall burn incense upon it.

And when Aaron lighteth the lamps at even, he shall burn incense upon it, a perpetual incense before the Lord throughout your generations.

Ye shall offer no strange incense thereon, nor burnt sacrifice, nor meat offering; neither shall ye pour drink offering thereon.

And Aaron shall make an atonement upon the horns of it once in a year with the blood of the sin offering of atonements: once in the year shall he make atonement upon it throughout your generations: it is most holy unto the Lord. (Exod. 30:1–10)

LOCATION OF THE ALTAR OF INCENSE

Place it before the veil that is by the ark of testimony, before the mercy seat that is over the testimony, where I will meet with you. (Exod. 30:6)

THE INGREDIENTS FOR MAKING THE INCENSE FOR THE ALTAR OF INCENSE

> *And the Lord said unto Moses, Take unto thee sweet spices, stacte, and onycha, and galbanum; these sweet spices with pure frankincense: of each shall there be a like weight:*
>
> *And thou shalt make it a perfume, a confection after the art of the apothecary, tempered together, pure and holy.*
>
> *And thou shalt beat some of it very small, and put of it before the testimony in the tabernacle of the congregation, where I will meet with thee: it shall be unto you most holy.*
>
> *And as for the perfume which thou shalt make, ye shall not make to yourselves according to the composition thereof: it shall be unto thee holy for the Lord.*
>
> *Whosoever shall make like unto that, to smell thereto, shall even be cut off from his people.* (Exod. 30:34–38)

The altar is a place of intercession. The priest was only permitted to go behind that veil once a year. Yet he was expected to intercede throughout the year—thus, the altar of incense.

The words spoken at the altar of incense should be a sweet savor unto God, as the incense was made of specific sweet smelling spices with a specific amounts of each.

> *Lord, I cry unto thee: make haste unto me; give ear unto my voice, when I cry unto thee.*
>
> *Let my prayer be set forth before thee as incense; and the lifting up of my hands as the evening sacrifice.* (Ps. 141:1–2)

> *Ointment and perfume rejoice the heart: so doth*
> *the sweetness of a man's friend by hearty counsel.*
> (Prov. 27:9)

An example of hearty counsel is seen when Jonathan, Saul's son, goes to David, who is hiding from Saul, and Jonathan encourages David with sweet words.

> *And Jonathan Saul's son arose, and went to David*
> *into the wood, and strengthened his hand in God.*
> *And he said unto him, Fear not: for the hand of*
> *Saul my father shall not find thee; and thou shalt*
> *be king over Israel, and I shall be next unto thee;*
> *and that also Saul my father knoweth.* (1 Sam.
> 23:16–17)

Moses intercedes for the people when God becomes so angry that He is about to kill them. Moses uses the very words God had spoken Himself and encourages God not to destroy the people for His namesake.

> *And Moses besought the Lord his God, and said,*
> *Lord, why doth thy wrath was hot against thy*
> *people, which thou hast brought forth out of the*
> *land of Egypt with great power, and with a mighty*
> *hand?*
> *Wherefore should the Egyptians speak, and*
> *say, For mischief did He bring them out, to slay*
> *them in the mountains, and to consume them from*
> *the face of the earth? Turn from thy fierce wrath,*
> *and repent of this evil against thy people.*
> *Remember Abraham, Isaac, and Israel, thy*
> *servants, to whom thou swearest by thine own self,*
> *and saidst unto them, I will multiply your seed as*

> *the stars of heaven, and all this land that I have*
> *spoken of will I give unto your seed, and they shall*
> *inherit it forever.*
> *And the Lord repented of the evil which He*
> *thought to do unto His people.* (Exod. 32:11–14)

The altar of incense being transported with staves by the priests means that the minister of the gospel is responsible for knowing how to come before God to intercede for others.

Just as at the brazen altar the priest placed the sacrifices upon the altar, we understand that the sacrifices are not the animal, but specific words spoken by the priests at the altar of incense. Sacrifices made on both the burnt altar and the altar of incense produce a sweet savor unto the Lord, but they are different. The sacrifices made on the burnt altar represent vows, confessions, renouncements, and forgiveness for sins. But the incense on the altar of incense is the sweet perfume from a pure heart, giving adoration to Him.

> *But Aaron and his sons offered upon the altar of*
> *the burnt offering, and on the altar of incense,*
> *and were appointed for all the work of the place*
> *most holy, and to make an atonement for Israel,*
> *according to all that Moses the servant of God had*
> *commanded.* (1 Chron. 6:49)

Zacharias the father of John prayed in intercession at the altar of incense:

> *And it came to pass, that while he executed the*
> *priest's office before God in the order of his course,*
> *According to the custom of the priest's office,*
> *his lot was to burn incense when he went into the*
> *temple.*

> *And the whole multitude of the people were praying without at the time of incense.* (Luke 1:8–10)

> *For from the rising of the sun even unto the going down of the same my name shall be great among the Gentiles; and in every place incense shall be offered unto my name, and a pure offering: for my name shall be great among the heathen, saith the Lord of hosts.* (Mal. 1:11)

God commands an offering of incense not just in the Old Testament, but also in the New Testament. In His instructions He says the words "throughout your generations," which means forever.

In the beginning of the book of Revelation, John was told that what he was about to see were things that are about to happen, not things from the past:

> *And when He had taken the book, the four beasts and the four and twenty elders fell down before the Lamb, having every one of them harps, and golden vials full of odors, which are the prayers of saints.* (Rev. 5:8)

> *And when he had opened the seventh seal, there was silence in heaven about the space of half an hour.*
> *And I saw the seven angels which stood before God; and to them were given seven trumpets.*
> *And another angel came and stood at the altar, having a golden censer; and there was given unto him much incense, that he should offer it with the prayers of the saints upon the golden altar which was before the throne.*

And the smoke of the incense, which came with the prayers of the saints, ascended up before God out of the angel's hand.

And the angel took the censer, and filled it with fire of the altar, and cast it into the earth: and there were voices, and thunderings, and lightnings, and an earthquake. (Rev. 8:1–5)

CHAPTER NINE

THE ARK OF THE COVENANT AND THE MERCY SEAT

This study is about the ark of the covenant and the mercy seat, but before we go to the mercy seat, we must address the veil between the altar of incense and the ark.

> *And thou shalt make a veil of blue, and purple, and scarlet, and fine twined linen of cunning work: with cherubims shall it be made:*
>
> *And thou shalt hang it upon four pillars of shittim wood overlaid with gold: their hooks shall be of gold, upon the four sockets of silver.*
>
> *And thou shalt hang up the veil under the tacks, that thou mayest bring in thither within the veil the ark of the testimony: and the veil shall divide unto you between the Holy Place and the Most Holy.* (Exod. 26:31–33)

The veil separated the altar of incense, which was located in the Holy Place, from the mercy seat, which was in the Holy of Holies. The veil was a reminder and a warning to the high priest to make sure the atonement was accepted at the burnt altar and he had washed himself of the blood of the sacrifice he had caught in the basin, for he had to be sanctified, holy, before entering.

Although it is not recorded in the Bible, a rope was attached to the ankle of the high priest before he went into the Holy of Holies so that he could be pulled out if he died while in the room. The hem of his garment had bells and pomegranates that made sounds as he walked. If his stay was prolonged and the congregation did not hear the sound of the bells, his dead body was pulled out.

The veil was wrought with cherubim (2 Chron. 3:14), just as cherubim were placed at the entrance of the Garden of Eden to keep the way of the Tree of Life.

Before Christ, only the high priests could enter into the Holy of Holies, and they entered once a year to offer atonement for the people. But when Jesus died on the cross, the veil of the temple was rent from the top to the bottom. When He rose, He took His own blood before the throne of the Father to present the atonement once and for all. He did this after He spoke to Mary Magdalene, saying, "Touch me not; for I am not yet ascended to my Father: but go to my brethren, and say unto them, I ascend unto my Father, and your Father; and to my God, and your God" (John 20:17). He was fulfilling the responsibility of the high priest.

The first veil represents the separation between God and man because of man's sin. The second veil represents separation between God and man because of man's lack of knowledge of God, His ways, and His heart.

> *And not as Moses, which put a veil over his face,*
> *that the children of Israel could not steadfastly look*
> *to the end of that which is abolished:*
>
> *But their minds were blinded: for until this*
> *day remaineth the same veil untaken away in the*
> *reading of the Old Testament; which veil is done*
> *away in Christ.*

> *But even unto this day, when Moses is read, the
> veil is upon their heart.*
> *Nevertheless when it shall turn to the Lord, the
> veil shall be taken away.* (2 Cor. 3:13–16)

> *And He will destroy in this mountain the face of
> the covering cast over all people, and the veil that
> is spread over all nations.* (Isa. 25:7)

Although Jesus removed the veil through His ministry and spreading the understanding of God's word, it is up to every man to attain understanding it for himself. John the Revelator called that veil a seal that covered the little book.

> *And I saw in the right hand of Him that sat on the
> throne a book written within and on the backside,
> sealed with seven seals.*
> *And I saw a strong angel proclaiming with a
> loud voice, Who is worthy to open the book, and
> to loose the seals thereof?*
> *And no man in heaven, nor in earth, neither
> under the earth, was able to open the book, neither
> to look thereon.*
> *And I wept much, because no man was found
> worthy to open and to read the book, neither to
> look thereon.*
> *And one of the elders saith unto me, Weep not:
> behold, the Lion of the tribe of Judah, the Root of
> David, hath prevailed to open the book, and to
> loose the seven seals thereof.* (Rev. 5:1–5)

Every born-again believer is responsible for taking the book to gain understanding of God's righteousness, His ways, and His heart.

And the voice which I heard from heaven spake unto me again, and said, Go and take the little book which is open in the hand of the angel which standeth upon the sea and upon the earth.

And I went unto the angel, and said unto him, Give me the little book. And he said unto me, Take it, and eat it up; and it shall make thy belly bitter, but it shall be in thy mouth sweet as honey.

And I took the little book out of the angel's hand, and ate it up; and it was in my mouth sweet as honey: and as soon as I had eaten it, my belly was bitter.

And he said unto me, Thou must prophesy again before many peoples, and nations, and tongues, and kings. (Rev. 10:8–11)

THE ARK AND THE MERCY SEAT

And they shall make an ark of shittim wood. . . .

And thou shalt put into the ark the testimony with I shall give thee.

And thou shalt make a mercy seat of pure gold: two cubits and a half shall be the length thereof, and a cubit and a half the breadth thereof.

And thou shalt make two cherubims of gold, of beaten work shalt thou make them, in the two ends of the mercy seat.

And make one cherub on the end, and the other cherub on the other end: even of the mercy seat shall ye make the cherubims on the two ends thereof.

And the cherubims shall stretch forth their wings on high, covering the mercy seat with their

wings, and their faces shall look one to another;
toward the mercy seat shall the faces of the
cherubims be.

And thou shalt put the mercy seat above upon
the ark; and in the ark thou shalt put the testimony
that I shall give thee.

And there I will meet with thee, and I will
commune with thee from above the mercy seat,
from between the two cherubims which are upon
the ark of the testimony, of all things which I will
give thee in commandment unto the children of
Israel. (Exod. 25:10–22)

The ark represents the very presence of God. The presence of God was with the children of Israel always: when they traveled, when they sojourned, even when they went to war, the ark of God was taken with them. Before the children of Israel crossed the Jordan, the priests carrying the ark had to step into the water first to open the way.

So the people went to Shiloh, that they might bring
from thence the ark of the covenant of the Lord of
hosts, which dwelleth between the cherubims: and
the two sons of Eli, Hophni and Phinehas, were
there with the ark of the covenant of God.

And when the ark of the covenant of the Lord
came into the camp, all Israel shouted with a great
shout, so that the earth rang again.

And when the Philistines heard the noise of the
shout, they said, What meaneth the noice of this
great shout in the camp of the Hebrews? And they
understood that the ark of the Lord was come into
the camp. (1 Sam. 4:4–6)

Behold, the ark of the covenant of the Lord of all the earth passeth over before you into Jordan.

Now therefore take you twelve men out of the tribes of Israel, out of every tribe a man.

And it shall come to pass, as soon as the soles of the feet of the priests that bear the ark of the Lord, the Lord of all the earth, shall rest in the waters of Jordan, that the waters of Jordan shall be cut off from the waters that come down from above; and they shall stand upon an heap. (Josh. 3:11–13)

Now Jericho was straitly shut up because of the children of Israel: none went out, and none came in.

And the Lord said unto Joshua, See, I have given into thine hand Jericho, and the king thereof, and the mighty men of valor.

And ye shall compass the city, all ye men of war, and go round about the city once. Thus shalt thou do six days.

And seven priests shall bear before the ark seven trumpets of rams' horns: and the seventh day ye shall compass the city seven times, and the priests shall blow with the trumpets.

And it shall come to pass, that when they make a long blast with the ram's horn, and when ye hear the sound of the trumpet, all the people shall shout; and the wall of the city shall fall down flat, and the people shall ascend up every man straight before him. (Josh. 6:1-5)

God will not tolerate the priest carrying the ark of God representing His presence to carry it improperly. The priests were responsible for being sanctified before transporting the ark; they had to live a life of holiness and know the proper manner in which

God commanded them to carry it. Responsibility is the meaning of the priests bearing the ark on their shoulders.

It is because of the sins of Hophni and Phinehas, the sons of Eli the high priest, who have no respect for God and carry the ark of God into the camp, that when Israel goes out to fight, God causes the army of Israel to lose the battle, and the ark of God is taken by the Philistines.

> *And the Philistines fought, and Israel was smitten, and they fled every man into his tent: and there was a very great slaughter; for there fell of Israel thirty thousand footmen.*
>
> *And the ark of God was taken; and the two sons of Eli, Hophni and Phinehas, were slain.* (1 Sam 4:10–11)

It is because the priests aren't aware that they are supposed to be sanctified, nor do they know that they are supposed to carry the ark upon their shoulders, that the young priest Uzzah dies.

> *And they set the ark of God upon a new cart, and brought it out of the house of Abinadab that was in Gibeah: and Uzzah and Ahio, the sons of Abinadab, drove the new cart.*
>
> *And they brought it out of the house of Abinadab which was in Gibeah, accompanying the ark of God: and Ahio went before the ark.*
>
> *And David and all the house of Israel played before the Lord on all manner of instruments made of fir wood, even on harps, and on psalteries, and on timbrels, and on cornets, and on cymbals.*
>
> *And when they came to Nachon's threshing floor, Uzzah put forth his hand to the ark of God, and took hold of it; for the oxen shook it.*

> *And the anger of the Lord was kindled against Uzzah; and God smote him there for his error: and there he died by the ark of God.* (2 Sam. 6:3–7)

All ministers of the gospel, particularly pastors, are responsible for knowing the proper manner of carrying the presence of God and knowing due order, which means each one has read and studied the five books of Moses, especially Exodus and Leviticus.

The name Leviticus means "instructions to the priests"; every minister of the gospel of Jesus Christ is responsible for knowing how to minister at the burnt altar and the meaning of the five sacrifices.

Many say we don't need to know this because that is Old Testament, and under the New Testament we minister as Jesus ministered. But Jesus ministered according to the priests in the Old Testament. It was the only testament He had; there was no New Testament.

Every Jewish young man was required to know the five books of Moses and be able to recite them by the time they were twelve years old, including Jesus.

> *And when He was twelve years old, they went up to Jerusalem after the custom of the feast.*
>
> *And when they had fulfilled the days, as they returned, the child Jesus tarried behind in Jerusalem; and Joseph and His mother knew not of it.*
>
> *But they, supposing Him to have been in the company, went a day's journey: and they sought Him among their kinsfolk and acquaintance.*
>
> *And when they found Him not, they turned back again to Jerusalem, seeking Him.*
>
> *And it came to pass, that after three days they found Him in the temple, sitting in the midst of*

*the doctors, both hearing them, and asking them
questions.*

*And all that heard Him were astonished at His
understanding and answers.* (Luke 2:42–47)

God is a God of order, His order: everything must be done
according to His requirements, as Jesus says in Matthew 6,
according to the righteousness of God. The tabernacle and its
ministry are still the same—not the building or the sacrificing
of animals, but the meaning behind the tabernacle, its vessels, its
ministry, and the process of sacrificing animals. God admonishes
Moses to make it according to the pattern he has seen in the
mount. To admonish means to warn. He warns Moses not to vary
from the pattern.

*Who serve unto the example and shadow of
heavenly things, as Moses was admonished of God
when he was about to make the tabernacle: for, See,
saith He, that thou make all things according to the
pattern showed thee in the mount.*

*But now hath He obtained a more excellent
ministry, by how much also He is the mediator of a
better covenant, which was established upon better
promises.* (Heb. 8:5–6)

The law of God was not done away with, but the law of sin
and death: if a man sinned, he died. When Jesus died on the cross,
the execution of the law by sacrificing an animal changed in that
Jesus became that sacrifice once and for all. Instead of killing an
animal, God requires man instead to make confessions and mean
it from his heart.

*O Israel, return unto the Lord thy God; for thou
hast fallen by thine iniquity.*

91

> *Take with you words, and turn to the Lord: say*
> *unto Him, Take away all iniquity, and receive us*
> *graciously: so will we render the calves of our lips.*
> (Hos. 14:1–2)

The prophets in the Old Testament understood the new and living way.

> *Hear, O my people, and I will speak; O Israel, and*
> *I will testify against thee: I am God, even thy God.*
> *I will not reprove thee for thy sacrifices or thy*
> *burnt offerings, to have been continually before me.*
> *I will take no bullock out of thy house, nor he*
> *goats out of thy folds.*
> *For every beast of the forest is mine, and the*
> *cattle upon a thousand hills.*
> *I know all the fowls of the mountains: and the*
> *wild beasts of the field are mine.*
> *If I were hungry, I would not tell thee: for the*
> *world is mine, and the fullness thereof.*
> *Will I eat the flesh of bulls, or drink the blood*
> *of goats?*
> *Offer unto God thanksgiving; and pay thy vows*
> *unto the most High:*
> *And call upon me in the day of trouble: I will*
> *deliver thee, and thou shalt glorify me.* (Ps. 50:7–15)

> *If we say that we have no sin, we deceive ourselves,*
> *and the truth is not in us.*
> *If we confess our sins, He is faithful and just to*
> *forgive us our sins, and to cleanse us from all*
> *unrighteousness.*
> *If we say that we have not sinned, we make Him*
> *a liar, and His word is not in us.* (1 John 1:8–10)

CHAPTER TEN

THE MINISTRY OF CHERUBIM

What is the ministry of cherubim?

WHO ARE THE CHERUBIM?

The cherubim are spoken of in several books of the Bible. In Ezekiel 1 and 10, as well as in Revelation chapter 1, the writers give us detailed descriptions of the cherubim. Ezekiel calls them living creatures, but in chapter 10, he calls them cherubim. In the book of Revelation, John calls them beasts.

There is a very brief description in Isaiah 6. He calls them seraphim, but if you pay close attention to his description, except for the six wings, the description aligns with those of Ezekiel and John in the book of Revelation.

They stand around or by the throne of God; they have wings; they have the appearance of fire; they have chariots with wheels. Below I list the different aspects of their ministry.

They may be angels, but we also find evidence that they are worshippers of God:

> *Above it stood the seraphims: each one had six wings; with twain he covered his face, and with twain he covered his feet, and with twain he did fly.*
>
> *And one cried unto another, and said, Holy, holy, holy, is the Lord of hosts: the whole earth is full of His glory.* (Isa. 6:2–3)
>
> *And the four beasts had each of them six wings about him; and they were full of eyes within: and they rest not day and night, saying, Holy, holy, holy, Lord God Almighty, which was, and is, and is to come.* (Rev. 4:8)

They stand before the throne of God, and they carry the presence of God:

> *And the likeness of the firmament upon the heads of the living creature was as the color of the terrible crystal, stretched forth over their heads above.*
>
> *And under the firmament were their wings straight, the one toward the other: every one had two, which covered on this side, and every one had two, which covered on that side, their bodies.*
>
> *And when they went, I heard the noise of their wings, like the noise of great waters, as the voice of speech, as the noise of a host: when they stood, they let down their wings.*
>
> *And there was a voice from the firmament that was over their heads, when they stood, and had let down their wings.*
>
> *And above the firmament that was over their heads was the likeness of a throne, as the appearance of a sapphire stone: and upon the likeness as the appearance of a man above upon it.* (Ezek. 1:22—26)

When they move as they carry the presence of God, there appears a whirlwind, fire, chariots, and horses.

> *And it came to pass, as they still went on, and talked, that, behold, there appeared a chariot of fire, and horses of fire, and parted them both asunder; and Elijah went up by a whirlwind into heaven.*
>
> *And Elisha saw it, and he cried, My father, my father, the chariot of Israel, and the horsemen thereof. And he saw him no more: and he took hold of his own clothes, and rent them in two pieces.* (2 Kings 2:11–12)

> *And I looked, and, behold, a whirlwind came out of the north, a great cloud, and a fire infolding itself, and a brightness was about it, and out of the midst thereof as the color of amber, out of the midst of the fire.*
>
> *Also out of the midst thereof came the likeness of four living creatures. And this was their appearance: they had the likeness of a man.* (Ezek. 1:4–5)

> *As for the likeness of the living creatures, their appearance was like burning coals of fire, and like the appearance of lamps: it went up and down among the living creatures: and the fire was bright, and out of the fire went forth lightning.* (Ezek. 1:13)

They intercede for the people:

> *And I fell down before the Lord, as at the first, forty days and forty nights: I did neither eat bread,*

nor drink water, because of all your sins which ye sinned, in doing wickedly in the sight of the Lord, to provoke Him to anger.

For I was afraid of the anger and hot displeasure, wherewith the Lord was wroth against you to destroy you. But the Lord hearkened unto me at that time also.

And the Lord was very angry with Aaron to have destroyed him: and I prayed for Aaron also the same time. (Deut. 9:18–20)

And it come to pass at the time of the offering of the evening sacrifice, that Elijah the prophet came near, and said, Lord God of Abraham, Isaac, and Israel, let it be known this day that thou art God in Israel, and that I am thy servant, and that I have done all these things at thy word.

Hear me, O Lord, hear me, that this people may know that thou art the Lord God, and that thou hast turned their heart back again.

Then the fire of the Lord fell, and consumed the burnt sacrifice, and the wood, and the stones, and the dust, and licked up the water that was in the trench. (1 Kings 18:36–38)

And Zadok the priest, and his brethren the priests, before the tabernacle of the Lord in the high place that was at Gibeon,

To offer burnt offerings unto the Lord upon the altar of the burnt offering continually morning and evening, and to do according to all that is written in the law of the Lord, which He commanded Israel. (1 Chron. 16:39–40)

I pray for them: I pray not for the world, but for them which thou hast given me; for they are thine.

And all mine are thine, and thine are mine; and I am glorified in them. (John 17:9–10)

Neither pray I for these alone, but for them also which shall believe on me through their word;

That they all may be one: as thou, Father, art in me, and I in thee, that they also may be one in us: that the world may believe that thou hast sent me. (John 17:20–21)

Who is he that condemneth? It is Christ that died, yea rather, that is risen again, who is even at the right hand of God, who also maketh intercession for us. (Rom. 8:34)

They only went where the Spirit of God sent them:

And the word of the Lord came unto him [Elijah], saying,

Arise, get thee to Zarephath, which belongeth to Zidon, and dwell there: behold, I have commanded a widow woman there to sustain thee.

So he arose and went to Zarephath. And when he came to the gate of the city, behold, the widow woman was there gathering of sticks: and he called her, and said, Fetch me, I pray thee, a little water in a vessel, that I may drink. (1 Kings 17:8–10)

And the same day, when the even was come, He saith unto them, Let us pass over unto the other side. (Mark 4:35)

He left Judea, and departed again into Galilee.

And He must needs go through Samaria.

Then cometh He to a city of Samaria, which is called Sychar, near to the parcel of ground that Jacob gave to his son Joseph.

Now Jacob's well was there. Jesus therefore, being wearied with His journey, sat thus on the well: and it was about the sixth hour. (John 4:3–6)

Now when they had gone throughout Phrygia and the region of Galatia, and were forbidden of the Holy Ghost to preach the word in Asia,

After they were come to Mysia, they attempted to go into Bithynia: but the Spirit suffered them not. (Acts 16:6–7)

They only did what God commanded them to do:

And it came to pass after many days, that the word of the Lord came to Elijah in the third year, saying, Go, show thyself unto Ahab; and I will send rain upon the earth.

And Elijah went to show himself unto Ahab. And there was a sore famine in Samaria. (1 Kings 18:1–2)

And the Lord said unto him [Elijah], Go, return on thy way to the wilderness of Damascus: and when thou comest, anoint Hazael to be king over Syria:

And Jehu the son of Nimshi shalt thou anoint to be king over Israel: and Elisha the son of Shaphat of Abelmeholah shalt thou anoint to be prophet in thy room.

And it shall come to pass, that him that escapeth the sword of Hazael shall Jehu slay: and him that escapeth from the sword of Jehu shall Elisha slay.

Yet I have left me seven thousand in Israel, all the knees which have not bowed unto Baal, and every mouth which hath not kissed him.

So he departed thence, and found Elisha the son of Shaphat, who was plowing with twelve yoke of oxen before him, and he with the twelfth: and Elijah passed by him, and cast his mantle upon him. (1 Kings 19:15–19)

Then answered Jesus and said unto them, Verily, verily, I say unto you, The Son can do nothing of Himself, but what He seeth the Father do: for what things soever He doeth, these also doeth the Son likewise.

For the Father loveth the Son, and showeth Him all things that Himself doeth: and He will show Him greater works than these, that ye may marvel.

For as the Father raiseth up the dead, and quickeneth them; even so the Son quickeneth whom He will. (John 5:19–21)

They are witnesses, sometimes called the two olive trees, two candlesticks, or two anointed ones, and they stand before the throne of God.

And Elijah the Tishbite, who was of the inhabitants of Gilead, said unto Ahab, As the Lord God of Israel liveth, before whom I stand, there shall not be dew nor rain these years, but according to my word. (1 Kings 17:1)

And the angel of the Lord protested unto Joshua, saying,

Thus saith the Lord of hosts; If thou wilt walk in my ways, and if thou keep my charge, then thou shalt also judge my house, and shalt also keep my courts, and I will give thee places to walk among these that stand by. (Zech. 3:6–7)

Then answered I, and said unto him, What are these two olive trees upon the right side of the candlestick and upon the left side thereof?

And I answered again, and said unto him, What be these two olive branches which through the two golden pipes empty the golden oil out of themselves?

And he answered me and said, Knowest thou not what these be? And I said, No, my lord.

Then said he, these are the two anointed ones, that stand by the Lord of the whole earth. (Zech. 4:11–14)

And I will give power unto my two witnesses, and they shall prophesy a thousand two hundred and threescore days, clothed in sackcloth.

These are the two olive trees, and the two candlesticks standing before the God of the earth.

And if any man will hurt them, fire proceedeth out of their mouth, and devoreth their enemies: and if any man will hurt them, he must in this manner be killed.

These have power to shut heaven, that it rain not in the days of their prophecy: and have power over waters to turn them to blood, and to smite the earth with all plagues, as often as they will. (Rev. 11:3-6)

Their ministry can be seen in Moses and Elijah; we know that Elijah stopped the rain, and Moses turned water into blood.

They were kings, priests, ordinary men, and prophets. Ezekiel called them creatures in chapter eleven, and cherubim in chapter ten; but John called them beasts in Revelation 4:6–9. Both men describe each of them as having four faces: the face of a lion, the face of a calf or ox, the face of a man, and the face of an eagle.

The face of a lion represents the King, the Lion of the tribe of Judah (Gen. 49:9–10; Rev. 5:5). The calf or ox represents a priest (Deut. 25:4; 1 Cor. 9:9). The man represents the Son of Man (Eze. 37:3; Matt. 9:6). The face of an eagle represents a prophet because of his sight (Hosea 8:1).

> *And before the throne there was a sea of glass like unto crystal: and in the midst of the throne, and round about the throne, were four beasts full of eyes before and behind.*
>
> *And the first beast was like a lion, and the second beast like a calf, and the third beast had a face as a man, and the fourth beast was like a flying eagle.*
>
> *And the four beasts had each of them six wings about him; and they were full of eyes within: and they rest not day and night, saying, Holy, holy, holy, Lord God Almighty, which was, and is, and is to come.* (Rev. 4:6–8)

> *As for the likeness of the living creatures, their appearance was like burning coals of fire, and like the appearance of lamps: it went up and down among the living creatures; and the fire was bright, and out of the fire went forth lightning.* (Ezek. 1:13)

CHAPTER ELEVEN

THE GARMENT OF THE PRIESTS

And these are the garments which they shall make;
a breastplate and an ephod, and a robe, and an
embroidered coat, a miter, and a girdle; and they
shall make holy garments for Aaron thy brother,
and his sons, that he may minister unto me in the
priest's office. (Exod. 28:4)

The high priest wore the sacred linen pants, a belt, a blue robe, and an ephod placed over the robe, as well as a breastplate fastened to the ephod. He also wrapped his head with a turban and tied a crown on his forehead. When conducting the temple services, the high priest had to remain barefoot.

The high priest wore no shoes or sandals while he ministered. He walked barefooted on the dirt floor of the tabernacle and the temple. This is because the floor of both the tabernacle and the temple complex were sanctified, made holy. He had washed his feet before entering, removing even the sin and dust of the world.

His clothing signified that nothing should come between the priests and the holiness of God, lest it should make the service invalid.

The clothing of the other priests, the Levites, were the sacred linen pants, a linen tunic, and a belt. They also wore a covering for their heads.

The garments of the high priest are special, in that Aaron could not die until he removed them, signifying the responsibility of the high priest within his ministry. Only God can call one to this office.

> *For every high priest taken from among men is ordained for men in things pertaining to God, that he may offer both gifts and sacrifices for sins:*
>
> *Who can have compassion on the ignorant, and on them that are out of the way; for that he himself also is compassed with infirmity.*
>
> *And by reason hereof he ought, as for the people, so also for himself, to offer for sins.*
>
> *And no man taketh this honor unto himself, but he that is called of God, as was Aaron.* (Heb. 5:1–4)

> *I will greatly rejoice in the Lord, my soul shall be joyful in my God; for He hath clothed me with the garments of salvation, He hath covered me with the robe of righteousness, as a bridegroom decketh himself with ornaments, and as a bride adorneth herself with her jewels.* (Isa. 61:10)

The garment of the priest is the garment of salvation and righteousness; it is also called the whole armor and the bridal garment. The priest wears it both as a priest and a warrior. A disciple will not be sent forth to his ministry until they are well prepared by God. For the high priest must know and understand spiritual warfare, deliverance, healing, and salvation.

You should not say you have a ministry of just preaching of the gospel without knowing how to cast out demons and lay hands on the sick. Likewise, you cannot say you have a deliverance ministry and not know how to preach the gospel. To say such reveals your ignorance. They all go hand in hand.

Let me give you an example.

> *And he arose, and came to his father. But when he was yet a great way off, his father saw him, and had compassion, and ran, and fell on his neck, and kissed him.*
>
> *And the son said unto him, Father, I have sinned against heaven, and in thy sight, and am no more worthy to be called thy son.*
>
> *But the father said to his servants, Bring forth the best robe, and put it on him; and put a ring on his hand, and shoes on his feet:*
>
> *And bring hither the fatted calf, and kill it; and let us eat, and be merry.*
>
> *For this my son was dead, and is alive again; he was lost, and is found. And they began to be merry.*
> (Luke 15:20–24)

The gifts the father gives to his son have a special meaning and reveal the maturity of his son. For in his sin the younger son has learned and experienced righteousness and salvation. The robe given to him by his father represents the garment of salvation; the ring represents authority; the shoes represent the fact that the son has learned how to teach others the gospel of peace.

The younger son has sinned and experienced the mercy of God and his father after he returns and repents; that mercy is symbolized by the garment of salvation. He receives a ring, which is a sign of authority. Joseph receives the signet ring of Pharaoh, and Mordeica receives the signet ring of king Ahasuerus as a sign of authority. With the use of the signet ring, these men could decree a thing and seal it as if spoken by the king, and no man could reverse the decree.

Likewise, when a born-again child of God speaks what God has said, no man can change what He has spoken. For example, Elijah prophesies that it will not rain for three years, and it does not rain. Jesus gives authority to His disciples to heal, deliver, and bring salvation to others using His name.

The shoes given to the younger son represent the fact that he could operate with authority because he understood what it was like to be in sin, he understood what it means to repent, and he understood the love of God through the example of his father when he returned home. He was shod with the preparation of the gospel of peace.

Elisha receives this authority from God after He has walked with Elijah and seen him taken up. Neither of the other prophets from the schools receive this authority.

> *And it came to pass, as they still went on, and talked, that, behold, there appeared a chariot of fire, and horses of fire, and parted them both asunder; and Elijah went up by a whirlwind into heaven.*
>
> *And Elisha saw it, and he cried, My father, my father, the chariot of Israel, and the horsemen thereof. And he saw him no more: and he took hold of his own clothes, and rent them in two pieces.*
>
> *He took up also the mantle of Elijah that fell from him, and went back, and stood by the bank of Jordan;*
>
> *And he took the mantle of Elijah that fell from him, and smote the waters, and said, Where is the Lord God of Elijah? And when he also had smitten the waters they parted hither and thither: and Elisha went over.* (2 Kings 2:11–14)

This is a spiritual garment.

> *Finally, my brethren, be strong in the Lord, and in the power of His might.*
>
> *Put on the whole armor of God, that ye may be able to stand against the wiles of the devil.*
>
> *For we wrestle not against flesh and blood, but against principalities, against powers, against the rulers of the darkness of this world, against spiritual wickedness in high places.*
>
> *Wherefore take unto you the whole armor of God, that ye may be able to withstand in the evil day, and having done all, to stand.*
>
> *Stand therefore, having your loins girt about with truth and having on the breastplate of righteousness;*
>
> *And your feet shod with the preparation of the gospel of peace;*
>
> *Above all, taking the shield of faith, wherewith ye shall be able to quench all the fiery darts of the wicked.*
>
> *And take the helmet of salvation, and the sword of the Spirit, which is the word of God:*
>
> *Praying always with all prayer and supplication in the Spirit, and watching thereunto with all perseverance and supplication for all saints;*
>
> *And for me, that utterance may be given unto me, that I may open my mouth boldly, to make known the mystery of the gospel.*
>
> *For which I am an ambassador in bonds: that therein I may speak boldly, as I ought to speak.*
> (Eph. 6:10–20)

You cannot put upon yourself the garments of righteousness and salvation; they are anointings of God for those chosen by God. He anoints them to accomplish His will.

> *And it came to pass, when they were gone over, that Elijah said unto Elisha, Ask what I shall do for thee, before I be taken away from thee. And Elisha said, I pray thee, let a double portion of thy spirit be upon me.*
>
> *And he said, Thou hast asked a hard thing: nevertheless, if thou see me when I am taken from thee, it shall be so unto thee; but if not, it shall not be so.* (2 Kings 2:9–10)

> *The Spirit of the Lord God s upon me; because the Lord hath anointed me to preach good tidings unto the meek; He hath sent me to bind up the brokenhearted, to proclaim liberty to the captives, and the opening of the prison to them that are bound.* (Isa. 61:1)

> *The Spirit of the Lord is upon me, because He hath anointed me to preach the gospel to the poor; He hath sent me to heal the brokenhearted, to preach deliverance to the captives, and recovering of sight to the blind, to set at liberty them that are bruised.* (Luke 4:18)

It is our responsibility to prepare our hearts to be arrayed in this garment; it is only the Lord who will clothe us in it. Notice that it is not Aaron who puts the high priest garments upon himself, nor does he remove them. Likewise, Zechariah sees Joshua, the high priest, being clothed with the special garments of the high priest—all at the command of God.

And the Lord spake unto Moses and Aaron in mount Hor, by the coast of the land of Edom, saying,

Aaron shall be gathered unto his people: for he shall not enter into the land which I have given unto the children of Israel, because ye rebelled against my word at the water of Meribah.

Take Aaron and Eleazar his son, and bring them up unto mount Hor:

And strip Aaron of his garments, and put them upon Eleazar his son: and Aaron shall be gathered unto his people, and shall die there.

And Moses did as the Lord commanded: and they went up into the mount Hor in the sight of all the congregation.

And Moses stripped Aaron of his garments, and put them upon Eleazar his son; and Aaron died there in the top of the mount: and Moses and Eleazar came down from the mount. (Num. 20:23–28)

And He showed me Joshua the high priest standing before the angel of the Lord, and Satan standing at his right hand to resist him.

And the Lord said unto Satan, The Lord rebuke thee, O Satan; even the Lord that hath chosen Jerusalem rebuke thee: is not this a brand plucked out of the fire?

Now Joshua was clothed with filthy garments, and stood before the angel.

And he answered and spake unto those that stood before Him, saying, Take away the filthy garments from him. and unto him He said, Behold, I have caused thine iniquity to pass from thee, and I will clothe thee with change of raiment.

> *And I said, Let them set a fair miter upon his head. So they set a fair miter upon his head, and clothed him with garments. And the angel of the Lord stood by.*
>
> *And the angel of the Lord protested unto Joshua, saying,*
>
> *Thus saith the Lord of hosts; If thou wilt walk in my ways, and if thou wilt keep my charge, then thou shalt also judge my house, and shalt also keep my courts, and I will give thee places to walk among these that stand by.* (Zech. 3:1–7)

The office of the high priest is to be a mediator between God and man. Let us consider our spiritual armor to make sure we don't bring the filth of the world before the throne of God as we minister to Him and in intercession for the people.

CHAPTER TWELVE

JESUS, THE FULFILLMENT OF THE TABERNACLE AND THE LAW

Studying the tabernacle will help you understand the ways of God as He reveals His heart through the tabernacle. The laws given to Moses are the requirements of God for man's relationship to be restored with Him through repentance. The first vessel of the tabernacle expresses the repentance of man and God's mercy. Paul often uses the cross of Jesus and His name Christ as one and the same. What we do at the cross today is the same as Moses taught the children of Israel to do at the burnt altar.

The tabernacle building itself represents Jesus, the sacrifices of the tabernacle represent Jesus, every vessel in the tabernacle represents Jesus, the high priest represents Jesus, and the ministry of the high priest in the tabernacle represents the ministry of Jesus.

Jesus didn't come to destroy the tabernacle but to reveal a new and living way to accomplish the same work done through the tabernacle. Not only did He not destroy the law, but he in fact fulfills it.

> *Think not that I am come to destroy the law, or the*
> *prophets: I am not come to destroy, but to fulfill.*
> *For verily I say unto you, till heaven and earth*
> *pass, one jot or one tittle shall in no wise pass from*
> *the law, till all be fulfilled.* (Matt. 5:17–18)

The law was not done away with, nor was the covenant. The law was within the covenant. The covenant was new in that the manner in which man would receive it changed. Instead of it being written on stone, God will write it in our hearts.

> *But now hath He obtained a more excellent*
> *ministry, by how much also He is the mediator*
> *of a better covenant, which was established upon*
> *better promises.*
> *For if that first covenant had been faultless, then*
> *should no place have been sought for the second.*
> *For finding fault with them, He saith, Behold,*
> *the days come, saith the Lord, when I will make a*
> *new covenant with the house of Israel and with the*
> *house of Judah:*
> *Not according to the covenant that I made with*
> *their fathers in the day when I took them by the*
> *hand to lead them out of the land of Egypt; because*
> *they continued not in my covenant, and I regarded*
> *them not, saith the Lord.*
> *For this is the covenant that I will make with*
> *the house of Israel after those days, saith the Lord;*
> *I will put my laws into their hearts: and I will be to*
> *them a God, and they shall be to me a people:*
> *And they shall not teach every man his*
> *neighbor, and every man his brother, saying, Know*
> *the Lord: for all shall know me, from the least to*
> *the greatest.*

> *For I will be merciful to their unrighteousness,*
> *and their sins and their iniquities will I remember*
> *no more.*
>   *In that He saith, A new covenant, He hath*
> *made the first old. Now that which decayeth and*
> *waxed old is ready to vanish away.* (Heb. 8:6–13)

Jesus was filled with the Spirit of God, as were the prophets; for without this infilling of the Holy Spirit, these men would not have been able to understand the ways of God. The candlestick, which represents the Holy Spirit in the Holy Place, revealed the table of shewbread, which is the word of God. Without the light of the Holy Spirit, we would not receive the revelation of God's word.

David understands by revelation the tabernacle and its ministry because as he reads God's word, the Holy Spirit is upon him. So did Isaiah (Isaiah 61:1), Ezekiel (Ezek. 1:3-5), and Jesus (Luke 4:18).

> *All this, said David, the Lord made me understand*
> *in writing by His hand upon me, even all the works*
> *of the pattern.* (1 Chron. 28:19)

John the Revelator says, "I was in the Spirit on the Lord's day" (Rev. 1:!0), implying that the Spirit of God was upon him.

Through the law we became cursed; but Jesus redeemed us from the curse of the law and gave us the promise of the Spirit through faith. (Gal. 3:10–14).

Therefore, in faith we confess our sin and ask God for forgiveness. In faith we know that He accepts our confession and extends His mercy. In faith we confess rather than bringing an animal sacrifice and seeing fire come down from heaven to burn it up.

Your body becomes the temple of God, and your heart the seat upon which His Spirit sits. It's not about a tabernacle or temple building. It is about your heart and your mind. We are to cleanse our heart through repentance, to renew our minds with the word of God, and be transformed. It is only by this that we become the temple of God.

Paul said, "The eyes of your understanding being enlightened; that ye may know what is the hope of His calling, and what the riches of the glory of His inheritance in the saints" (Eph. 1:18). You then become a portable tabernacle.

> *Know ye not that ye are the temple of God, and that the Spirit of God dwelleth in you?* (1 Cor. 3:16)

Jesus came to give us an example of that which God created man to be.

> *And so it is written, The first man Adam was made a living soul; the last Adam was made a quickening spirit.* (1 Cor. 15:45)

> *Now of the things which we have spoken this is the sum: We have such a high priest, who is on the right hand of the throne of the Majesty in the heavens;*
>
> *A minister of the sanctuary, and of the true tabernacle, which the Lord pitched, and not man.*
>
> *For every high priest is ordained to offer gifts and sacrifices: wherefore it is of necessity that this man have somewhat also to offer.*
>
> *For if He were on earth, He should not be a priest, seeing that there are priests that offer gifts according to the law:*
>
> *Who serve unto the example and shadow of heavenly things, as Moses was admonished of God*

when he was about to make the tabernacle: for, See, saith He, that thou make all things according to the pattern showed to thee in the mount.

But now hath He obtained a more excellent ministry, by how much also He is the mediator of a better covenant, which was established upon better promises. (Heb. 8:1–6)

God desires a kingdom of priests.

Now therefore, if ye will obey my voice indeed, and keep my covenant, then ye shall be a peculiar treasure unto me above all people: for all the earth is mine.

And ye shall be unto me a kingdom of priests, and a holy nation. These are the words which thou shalt speak unto the children of Israel. (Exod. 19:5–6)

And they sung a new song, saying, Thou art worthy to take the book, and to open the seals thereof: for thou wast slain, and hast redeemed us to God by thy blood out of every kindred, and tongue, and people, and nation;

And hast made us unto our God kings and priests: and we shall reign on the earth. (Rev. 5:9–10)

Now let us compare the ministry of Jesus with the ministry of the priest in the tabernacle.

The writer of Hebrews says, "For every high priest is ordained to offer gifts and sacrifices" (Heb. 8:3), which means we must learn how to minister gifts and sacrifices as a high priest, as Jesus did.

We have to begin with the sacrifices. What are sacrifices?

115

Sacrifices are vows and confessions of sin we make to God in agreement with His will (like signing a contract). God is the author of the covenant or contract; therefore, He establishes what these vows and confessions will be. When the vows and confessions are made in the Old Testament, God requires that they be signed with blood; instead of the blood of the offeror, He allowed them to use the blood of certain animals as substitute.

There are five main sacrifices along with one other that was offered alongside four of the sacrifices: the whole burnt offering, the meat or grain offering, the peace offering, the sin offering, and the trespass offering. The meat offering and the drink offering were always offered with the burnt offering, the peace offering, the sin offering, and the trespass offering.

The type of animal was not determined by the type of sacrifice the offeror brought, but what he could afford. The animals God required were calves, lambs, goats, turtle doves, and pigeons. Any other animal was not accepted.

The instructions for the offering and what was required of the offeror at the burnt altar were short compared to the instructions for the priests, as the priests had more responsibility.

The Lord holds the priests responsible for knowing, understanding, and being able to carry out every part of the service of sacrifices. For example, the person was required to bring a sacrifice of the cattle, or the herd, or of the flock. It had to be without blemish, and he had to bring it of his own will to the door of the tabernacle of the congregation. He had to obey the instructions of the priest when asked why he had come, giving the animal to the priest to check for blemishes, lay his hands on the head of the animal, cut the animal's throat, and hold the animal until its blood had drained into the basin the priest held.

As discussed earlier, once the blood had drained into the basin, the animal was handed to another priest for them to flay, cut in pieces, and separate the parts, distinguishing which parts went on the burnt altar and which were burned outside the camp in a clean place. With the sin offering and the peace offering, the priest received a portion of that animal. The priest was responsible for knowing where to sprinkle the blood of the animal, whether around the burnt altar or the horns of incense, before the veil in front of the Holy of Holies, or on the mercy seat.

Often we see Jesus ask those who approached Him, "What do you want me to do for you?" That is the same as the priest in the temple saying, "What are you here for?"

We often see Jesus ministering to people and believe that He operates as a vigilante, going around healing every sick person He comes upon, casting out demons from every possessed person He meets. But that is not true.

Jesus ministers to those who are brought to Him by a parent, someone responsible for them, or a friend. He only goes to places God the Father tells Him to go to (see, for example, John 4:4; Mark 4:35–5:21). Notice that in Mark 4 and 5, after He has finished talking to the Gadarene demoniac, He then passes over again to the other side, where He had come from.

Take a look at the healing of Peter's mother-in-law. Matthew and Mark give us the impression that Jesus walks into the house and sees the woman lying sick of a fever, and He simply lays hands on her and she is healed. But upon closer inspection, in Luke 4, Luke reveals to us that when Jesus enters into the house, someone asks Him to come and heal the woman. Luke also reveals the fact that before He lays hands on her to lift her up, He commands the fever to leave her. Jesus prays for the woman because they came to Him and asked Him. This confirms James's words "Is any sick among you? Let him call for the elders of the church; and let them pray over him, anointing him with oil in the name of the Lord" (James 5:14–15).

It is the centurion who comes to Jesus and asks Him to pray for his servant in Matthew 8. It is the friends of a man with the palsy who bring the sick man to Jesus in Matthew 9. It is blind Bartimaeus who cries out to Jesus to heal his eyes in Mark 10. It is

Jesus's mother Mary who comes to Jesus and tells Him that they have no wine at the wedding feast in John 2.

In each case, Jesus fulfills the word spoken by God that He would deliver everyone who cried out to Him.

> *Thus saith the Lord the maker thereof, the Lord that formed it, to establish it; the Lord is His name;*
> *Call unto me, and I will answer thee, and show thee great and mighty things, which thou knowest not.* (Jer. 33:2–3)

> *And it shall come to pass, that whosoever shall call on the name of the Lord shall be delivered: for in mount Zion and in Jerusalem shall be deliverance, as the Lord hath said, and in the remnant whom the Lord shall call.* (Joel 2:32)

It does not make any difference whether you are Jew or Gentile, a believer or not; God is waiting on you to open your mouth and cry out to Him. He cannot go back on His word. He will either send someone to you, or He will lead you to a person who can answer your petition.

There are other times when Jesus goes to a person to minister to them. It would seem as though He simply goes on His own and sees a need, but at those times He is indeed sent by God.

The woman at the well in John 4 was one of cases; we know this because John writes, "And He must needs go through Samaria" (John 4:4). That woman had cried out to God.

In Mark 4 and 5, Jesus and His disciples cross the sea to the country of the Gadarenes. As they get off the ship, a man with unclean spirits so fierce that he had been often bound with chains comes to meet them, and even from afar, he bows down to worship Jesus. Jesus casts the demons out of the man and is told to leave the country by the residents of Gadara. Jesus and His disciples get back onto the ship and go right back to the place they had come from. The man had cried out to God.

In Luke 7, Jesus goes to a city called Nain with His disciples. As He comes near the gate of the city, they meet a funeral procession in which a dead man, the only son of his mother, is being taken to be buried. The man's mother, a widow, follows the casket weeping aloud. Jesus walks over to her and says, "Weep not." Then He goes to the casket and touches it, and those that bear the casket stop. Jesus then says, "Young man, I say unto thee, Arise" (Luke 7:14). And the young man rises up.

Jesus never does enter the city; He is sent there on a mission from the Father. God not only answers those who call upon His name, but He has a particular concern for the fatherless, widows, and strangers.

> *He doth execute the judgment of the fatherless and widow, and loveth the stranger, in giving him food and raiment.* (Deut. 10:18)

> *A Father to the fatherless, and a judge of the widows, is God in His holy habitation.* (Ps. 68:5)

> *The Lord preserveth the strangers; He relieveth the fatherless and widow: but the way of the wicked He turneth upside down.* (Ps. 146:9)

To further prove that Jesus was not a vigilante healer just healing anyone He happened to come across, let us look at Him minister to the man at the pool of Bethesda in John 5.

Jesus goes to the market pool in Bethesda because the Father has sent Him. He heals the man who has an infirmity and cannot walk. Afterward the man is walking through the temple carrying the bed he had lain on when the leaders of the temple rebuke him for carrying the bed on the Sabbath. He tells them that the man who healed him had told him to take up his bed and walk. Shortly after, Jesus comes and is rebuked by the leaders in the temple for telling the man to take up his bed on the Sabbath. This was His response:

> *But Jesus answered them, My Father worketh hitherto, and I work.* (John 5:17)

> *Then answered Jesus and said unto them, Verily, verily, I say unto you. The Son can do nothing of Himself, but what He seeth the Father do: for what things soever He doeth, these also doeth the Son likewise.*
> *For the Father loveth the Son, and showeth Him all things that Himself doeth: and He will show Him greater works than these, that ye may marvel.*
> *For as the Father raiseth up the dead, and quickeneth them; even so the Son quickeneth whom He will.* (John 5:19–21)

Jesus did not operate in ministry as a divine being, but as a man like us. He came to set an example for man of what it means to be a son of God on earth. He, as a man, was able to preach, teach, save, heal, and deliver because He operated in the gifts of the Spirit. When He ascended to heaven, Paul tells us that Jesus gave those gifts unto men.

> *But unto every one of us is given grace according to the measure of the gift of Christ.*
> *Wherefore He saith, When He ascended up on high, He led captivity captive, and gave gifts unto men.* (Eph. 4:7–8)

Jesus teaches the ministry of the Spirit, and Paul lists the gifts of the Spirit in I Corinthians 12.

> *Howbeit when He, the Spirit of truth, is come, He will guide you into all truth: for He shall not speak of Himself; but whatsoever he shall hear, that shall He speak: and He will show you things to come.*
>
> *He shall glorify me: for He shall receive of mine, and shall show it unto you.*
>
> *All things that the Father hath are mine: therefore said I, that He shall take of mine, and shall show it unto you. (John 16:13–15)*

> *Now there are diversities of gifts, but the same Spirit.*
>
> *And there are differences of administrations, but the same Lord.*
>
> *And there are diversities of operations, but it is the same God which worketh all in all.*
>
> *But the manifestation of the Spirit is given to every man to profit withal.*
>
> *For to one is given by the Spirit the word of wisdom; to another the word of knowledge by the same Spirit;*
>
> *To another faith by the same Spirit; to another the gifts of healing by the same Spirit;*
>
> *To another the working of miracles; to another prophecy; to another discerning of spirits; to another divers kinds of tongues; to another the interpretation of tongues:*
>
> *But all these worketh that one and the selfsame Spirit, dividing to every man severally as he will. (1 Cor. 12:4–11)*

He operated in the gifts as the Spirit of God led Him and was obedient unto the Father unto death, even the death of the cross.

> *Let this mind be in you, which was also in Christ Jesus:*
> *Who, being in the form of God, thought it not robbery to be equal with God.*
> *But made Himself of no reputation, and took upon Him the form of a servant, and was made in the likeness of men:*
> *And being found in fashion as a man, He humbled Himself, and became obedient unto death, even the death of the cross.* (Phil. 2:5–8)

To operate in these gifts, you must be a believer, be filled with the Holy Ghost, know how to hear the voice of God, have faith in God, and study God's word daily. Some of you will see in the Spirit, yet you still must know how to hear to receive understanding of what you see.

Each one of the gifts is given by the Spirit through hearing or seeing. But it is in faith the one seeing or hearing causes what you hear to manifest. In faith we speak that which we hear and or see. Faith cometh by hearing, and hearing by the word of God.

Jesus says He only does what He sees the Father doing (John 4:19–21). He also says He speaks only that which the Father commands Him to speak (John 12:49–50).

That is why Jesus marvels in Matthew 8, after the centurion, a Roman soldier, explains that he understands that Jesus does these miracles and healing because Jesus operates under the authority of God the Father. Jesus says He has not seen that type of faith in all Israel, meaning He had met no Israelite who understood the authority given to us by God.

Yes, we have been given dominion, authority, but we operate in authority according to the will of God.

> *And this is the confidence that we have in Him,*
> *that, if we ask any thing according to His will, He*
> *heareth us:*
>   *And if we know that He hear us, whatsoever*
> *we ask, we know that we have the petitions that we*
> *desired of Him.* (1 John 5:14–15)

If you are a minister of the gospel, especially a pastor of a church, you must recognize when people are in need of ministry. It may happen while you are in the pulpit, maybe in the middle of your sermon. It could happen while you're out shopping, talking on the phone, or visiting a friend.

Will you recognize the cry for help? They may not say the words *help me.* They may be using profane language, even cursing you, just like the man in Matthew 5. Will you recognize it?

I have seen individuals calling out for help during what we call testimony service, and the pastor or speaker is not in attendance, sometimes not even in the building. Sometimes the pastor was in the pulpit, but he didn't recognize the desperate cry of God's sheep.

I have seen demons manifest, interrupting the sermon; everyone would laugh, and the speaker would continue his message. The person left the building after the service with that same demon he came in with, plus an added one because the person lost hope.

I have seen the pastor give altar call; people came forward, some for salvation, some for healing. But the pastor only stood in the pulpit and said a general prayer, then sent the people back to their seats. Those seeking healing or deliverance returned to their seats knowing that they were not healed or delivered; those seeking salvation did not know whether they had received salvation or not.

I talked to a pastor about the altar call held during a revival service and asked him why the speaker said a general prayer instead of ministering to the people who came forward. He said he wanted to do more teaching before ministering to the people the following night. I said to him, "Then you should not have called them to the altar; they may not attend the service the following night or the rest of the week to hear your teaching."

We get so high minded to think it was our preaching is the reason the people come forward for salvation. When Jesus said, "No man can come to me, except the Father which hath sent me draw him" (John 6:44), God drew the person's heart to the altar. That person may not have heard a word the pastor spoke but had already talked with God before arriving; he was sitting there waiting for the altar call to give his life to Christ.

When you are outside the walls of the church building—on your job, in a park, on a bus, at the grocery store, or in a mall—will you recognize the cry of a lost sheep? Will you know how to minister to the person and place his sacrifice on the altar?

I knew of a believer in Christ who, while on his job, was approached by a friend. The friend asked him, "Man, I'm having problems with my wife; what should I do about it?" The Christian said to his friend, "Go home, kick the table over, and tell her that you are the man of that house." The friend went home, kicked the table over, yelled at his wife and said, "I am the man of this house!" The table hit the wife, and the husband ended up in court for domestic violence.

The Christian knew no more than he had been taught by the pastor of the church he attended. Yes, the husband is the head of his home; his first position is the high priest of his house, and as the high priest he is responsible for leading his family in prayer, especially when there is trouble in his home. Another name for a high priest is shepherd. A shepherd leads the sheep. If the shepherd is abusive, the sheep will scatter. God takes offense to those who scatter his sheep.

To know what to look for when ministering to people, we as ministers must know Jesus. In Jesus we find the first principles of the Oracles of God, we find the testimony of God, we find the promises of God, we find the instructions for the priest, and we learn how to carry out the instructions of God.

When we council people, what we say and how we say it must agree with the word of God, for He holds us responsible.

> *And ye shall know that I have sent this commandment unto you, that my covenant might be with Levi, saith the Lord of hosts.*
>
> *My covenant was with him of life and peace; and I gave them to him for the fear wherewith he feared me, and was afraid before my name.*
>
> *The law of truth was in his mouth, and iniquity was not found in his lips: he walked with me in peace and equity, and did turn many away from iniquity.*
>
> *For the priest's lips should keep knowledge, and they should seek the law at his mouth: for he is the messenger of the Lord of hosts.* (Mal. 2:4–7)

Let us pray!

Father God, search my heart. Reveal to me those things in which I am ignorant concerning Your word, Your ways, and Your righteousness. I confess them and ask You to forgive me. I rededicate my life to Jesus and ask Him to be my Lord and Savior. I ask that You fill me with Your Holy Spirit who will teach me to see and understand Your heart, Your ways, and Your will for my life.

Fill me with Your compassion for my brethren. Give me the knowledge I need to minister to them, that they too may come to know You as their heavenly Father. Give me wisdom to judge Your people as a minister of Your gospel, so that they turn their hearts to You. Give me a fresh hunger, thirst, and love for Your word and a desire to spend time alone with You every day. I want to know You; I want to know Your ways; I want to be with You forever! I thank You, Father!

In Jesus's name I pray. Amen.

Printed in the United States
by Baker & Taylor Publisher Services

Printed in the United States
by Baker & Taylor Publisher Services